A Kid's First Book of
BIRDWATCHING

SCOTT WEIDENSAUL

RUNNING PRESS
PHILADELPHIA
PENNSYLVANIA

A QUINTET BOOK

Text copyright © 1990 Quintet Publishing
Limited

First published in the United States of America
in 1990 by Running Press Book Publishers

ISBN 0-89471-826-6

9 8 7 6 5 4 3 2

Library of Congress Cataloguing in Publication Number 89-43598

This book was designed and produced by
Quintet Publishing Limited
6 Blundell Street
London N7 9BH

Creative Director: Peter Bridgewater
Art Director: Ian Hunt
Project Editor: David Game
Editor: Kate Chambers

Typeset in Great Britain by Central Southern
Typesetters, Eastbourne.
Manufactured in Hong Kong by Regent
Publishing Services Limited.
Printed in Hong Kong by Lee Fung Asco
Printers Limited, Hong Kong.

This book may be ordered by mail from the
publisher. Please add $2.50 for postage and
handling for each copy. But try your
book store first!
Running Press Book Publishers
125 South Tenty-second Street
Philadelphia, Pennsylvania 19103

Contents

Maps throughout this book show migratory patterns for each species: solid color indicates summer distribution, cross hatching, winter distribution, and the combination of the two shows all-year-round presence.

  SUMMER DISTRIBUTION

  WINTER DISTRIBUTION

  ALL YEAR DISTRIBUTION

Introduction

Birds are not the only animals to fly, although they are more closely associated with flight than any other group of creatures – from the fluttery wingbeats of a sparrow to the majestic soaring of a golden eagle.

How Birds Work

Every bird has feathers, its most important tools for flying. A feather is made of keratin, the same horny substance that your fingernails are made of. The quill is anchored in the skin, with small muscles that allow the bird to control its movement. Further up the shaft, thousands of interlocking barbules make up the soft part of the feather. Under a microscope, each barbule itself looks like an individual feather, with even smaller barbs, all covered with a series of minute hooks that hold the feather together.

A bird has several kinds of feathers. The largest are the flight feathers of the wings and tail; the outermost wing feathers are called *primaries*, while those closer to the body, which show when the wing is folded, are the *secondaries*. The wing feathers are stiff, and provide lift when the wing is flapped. The body is covered with smooth *contour feathers*, which streamline the bird in flight, while underneath the contour feathers are fluffy *down* feathers that trap air and keep the bird warm. The body feathers do not grow randomly on the bird's body, but sprout from distinct tracts, which you can see by gently parting a songbird's contour feathers.

A bird has other adaptations to life in the air. To reduce weight its bones are thin and hollow, reinforced with struts through the center. There are large air sacs through its body, and instead of heavy teeth, the bird has a strong, light beak of keratin. Its chest muscles are unusually large in comparison with its body size, to power the wings in flight, and to fuel this engine, birds ordinarily eat high-energy foods like insects, seeds and nectar.

FAR RIGHT: Song and color play a large part in courtship among birds. Here, a male red-winged blackbird sings his creaky *ok-a-lee-e-e-e* song from a conspicuous perch, while flashing his red-and-yellow wing patches.

RIGHT: A flock of Canada geese splashes down for a landing in a marshy pond. Birds are not the only animals that fly, but they are the most closely associated with the air.

Life History

All birds lay eggs, although the ways they court, nest and raise their young varies tremendously. Birds may attract their mates through visual displays (like the swooping dives of the red-tailed hawk) but more commonly by voice. A male bird's song is more than a pretty tune – it is how the bird attracts a female, defines its territory and keeps away rivals. A robin, singing *Bcheerily-cheeryup-cheerio* from a treetop, is telling all the other male robins within earshot that the tree is part of his property, and that if another male intrudes, he's in for a fight.

The song is also one way that a female has of judging how good a mate the male will be; if he sings poorly, or if his song is unusual, she may not choose him. In some species, though, originality is prized. Female mockingbirds usually choose the males with the largest number of songs, so male mockers steal tunes from many other birds to pad out their repertoire. (Songs should not be confused with calls, which are shorter, given by both sexes and have little to do with courtship. Calls are usually a means of communicating within a flock, such as warning of danger.)

Not every bird sings. The herring gull can only manage yelps and squeals, so to win a mate, the male goes through an elaborate series of displays. The cock ring-necked pheasant cackles loudly while flapping his wings, all the while showing off his brightly colored feathers.

Most birds build nests, though not all; the killdeer makes a scrape in the soil, and the great horned owl appropriates the nests of squirrels, crows or hawks. Even among species that do build nests, the size, shape and materials vary greatly. Woodpeckers chop holes in trees, while wood ducks use rotted cavities. Goldfinches build their nests of plant down covered with spider webs, while the mourning dove's shallow nest of twigs is so thin you can see the eggs through the bottom.

The eggs are laid one at a time, usually one per

day until the clutch is complete. Songbirds, waterfowl and gamebirds generally wait until the clutch is complete to start incubating the eggs, so all the chicks hatch at the same time, but hawks and owls begin as soon as the first is laid, so their chicks hatch over a period of days. A baby bird may be born blind, helpless and almost naked (as with most songbirds) or alert, covered with down and able to leave the nest almost immediately (as with gamebirds, shorebirds and waterfowl). Songbird chicks usually stay in the nest for about two weeks, fed every few minutes by their parents. Their feathers sprout quickly through their baby down, and for the last several days they spend much of their time exercising their wings. Once they leave the nest (an event called "fledging"), they still receive food and care from their parents for a few weeks more.

Some birds spend their entire lives within the same small area, winter and summer, but most are migratory, at least to a degree. Many of North America's songbirds are insect-eaters, and must retreat from the advance of winter. They travel vast distances each year, commuting between their breeding grounds in the U.S. and Canada, and wintering grounds in Mexico, Central and South America. Navigating with an instinctive knowledge of where they want to go, they use landmarks, the position of the sun, moon, and stars and the direction of the wind to find their way. The young of the year do not, as is often thought, follow older birds that have made the trip before — in many cases, the young migrate first, followed a few weeks later by their parents.

Their journeys can be long or short. In the western mountains, a bird's migration may be simply to fly from a high altitude to a low valley. On the other hand, some warblers take off from the coast of New England and fly, non-stop over the ocean, to the northern coast of South America, a journey of more than 2,000 miles.

Birding

Watching birds is a fascinating hobby that can last a lifetime — and take on many forms. Some birders specialize in combing the countryside for new species to add to their "life list" (a tally of all the birds they have ever seen), while others prefer to study the more common species, learning about their lives through patient observation. Some people specialize in watching hawks, or ducks, or songbirds, while others just enjoy feeding the birds each winter.

Birding doesn't require much in the way of equipment. A pair of binoculars are almost essential, especially for watching songbirds. Binoculars are rated by their magnification and field of view; the most common size are rated 7x35, which offer 7-power magnification and a reasonable field of view. Practice finding objects quickly through your binoculars; pick out a branch or a leaf, and — while not taking your eyes from it

— bring up the glasses smoothly. Being able to immediately spot a bird with the binoculars is invaluable with small, quick species like warblers.

Also get a good field guide that covers your part of the continent; several recommended guides are listed in the reference section at the end of this book. Most guides show paintings of the birds in all plumages, and point out the appropriate "field marks" — those aspects of color, shape, size or behavior that allow you to identify the species. Just as you recognize friends by the color of their hair and the shape of their faces, so too can you identify birds by noting such details. For example, the best field mark of an American robin is its brick-red breast, while the barn swallow's major field mark is its deeply forked tail — no other swallow has that feature.

Learn the field marks of the most common birds in your area, so that when you see an unfamiliar species in the field, you won't waste time thumbing frantically through a guide. Of course, you will sometimes see a bird that looks like nothing you've seen before. In such situations it is better to leave the guide in your pack and concentrate on the bird – does it have wingbars? An eye-ring? What is the shape of the bill? The length of the tail? Are there any distinctive features? A small notebook is handy for jotting down field marks, or even drawing very rough sketch. Later, compare your notes to the field guide to make an identification (and don't be too concerned if you are still puzzled – even the experts are stumped on occasion).

As you gain more experience in bird-watching, you may want to keep records, to remind you of good field trips, rare birds or unusual behavior. Over the years, careful observation by amateurs has unlocked many of the mysteries of bird life. Most birders keep a life list, recording where, when and under what circumstances they first saw a new species, but you can keep monthly lists, home property lists, trip lists, feeder lists – whatever your imagination suggests. Or try observing a pair of birds through their entire breeding cycle, from the beginnings of nest construction through the fledging of the chicks (do so at a distance, however, to avoid disturbing them unduly).

Birding can be done anywhere, and some of the most rewarding times afield may be in your own backyard. In the summer, nesting boxes will attract such cavity-dependent birds as eastern bluebirds, house wrens and black-capped chickadees; detailed plans for many different species are available from most state or provincial wildlife agencies, or from private conservation organizations. In the winter, a bird feeding station is an excellent way to help the birds and brighten a cold, dreary day. There are a wide variety of feeders on the market, but the most effective are usually simple plastic tube feeders hung from tree branches, and roofed tray feeders mounted on poles. By far the best food is plain sunflower seed, especially the all-black "oil" sunflower, which is

LEFT: Bird nests range from the simple to the complex. Typical is that of the song sparrow – a cup of woven grass hidden in thick cover on the ground.

ABOVE: Marshes, ponds and other wetlands are excellent destinations for bird-watching trips. Here, a male common grackle perches among pond lilies while looking for food.

smaller than gray-striped seed. Other good winter foods are finely cracked corn, white millet and suet (beef fat) hung in baskets for woodpeckers. Avoid supermarket seed mixes, which include a high proportion of waste seeds like rape, which birds do not eat.

As interesting as backyard birding can be, eventually you'll want to expand your horizons. To find new species, go to new habitats – to marshes and swamps for wading birds and waterfowl, or to mountains for deep-woods songbirds like vireos. Parks (even city parks) and nature reserves are especially good places to bird, because there are often marked trails that lead to the best spots, and there may even be guided bird walks that you can attend. While birding is often a solitary hobby, joining a group of more experienced birders is an excellent way to learn new techniques and see new species – perhaps birds you had overlooked before. Bird-watchers are among the friendliest people on earth, and are always happy to help out an excited beginner.

Canada Goose
BRANTA CANADENSIS

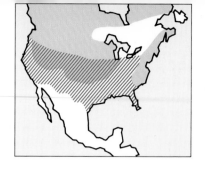

Flying high in their classic V-formation, Canada (not "Canadian") geese are a common sight in spring and fall all over North America. They are now common breeding birds in many areas, as well, so there is a good chance of seeing them in parks, lakes and along rivers at almost any time of the year.

A Canada goose is big, about twice as large as a mallard duck, with a long, black neck and head, brown body and a white chin patch that is its best field mark. In flight they do not always maintain a V; the flock may fly in a ragged line, a jumble or several smaller, overlapping Vs. On the ground or in the air, the geese honk almost constantly, a loud, two-note call: *har-RONK! har-RONK!*

In city parks and near picnic grounds, Canada geese can become very tame, begging for food from people, but in wilder places they are wary birds, difficult to get close to, especially in the breeding season. Geese mate for a long time, possibly for life, and the pair usually return to the same general area each year to nest. The female builds a mound of grasses, weeds and leaves, sometimes on top of a muskrat lodge that sticks up above the water. She lines the nest with soft down plucked from her breast, and lays between four and seven eggs, which she incubates for nearly a month.

When the chicks hatch they can walk, swim and feed themselves immediately, unlike the babies of songbirds like robins. The adult geese are very attentive parents, protecting their goslings from danger and leading them to the best food. Within several weeks the babies lose their yellow down and begin to grow their adult plumage, and by the end of the summer it is hard to tell the youngsters from the adults.

During the summer Canada geese graze on land plants like grass and clover, and feed on aquatic plants in shallow water. In winter they like corn and other grains left in the fields after harvest.

SPOTTER'S NOTES

● **Plumage** – Sexes identical. Brown body, black neck and head, white chin patch.

● **Size** – Varies; most 40–45 in (100–120 cms) long, but some western races only as big as a duck.

● **Behavior** – Forms big flocks, except in breeding season. Migrates in large numbers during spring and fall, honking loudly.

● **Habitat** – Wetlands – lakes, ponds, rivers, marshes, parks and golf courses.

IDENTIFICATION

● **Call** – Two-note honk: *har-RONK!*

● **Food** – Green plants, grains, seeds, some insects.

● **Nest** – Large mound of vegetation near water, lined with down.

● **Eggs** – 4–7; off-white.

Mallard
ANAS PLATYRHYNCHOS

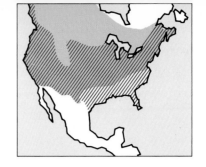

The mallard duck is probably one of the most widespread (and best-known) birds in the world. It is found in every part of North America except for the eastern arctic, and winters as far south as Florida and south Texas.

As with most ducks, the male and female are colored differently. The male (or drake) has a shiny green head, white neck ring, chestnut breast and gray body. The female (or hen) is mottled brown to help camouflage her on the nest. Both sexes have a bright blue wing patch with white edges called a speculum, and orange legs. In late summer the drake loses his brilliant colors for several weeks, and looks very much like the hen. The best way to tell such an "eclipse" drake is to look at the beak; a drake's is plain greenish-yellow, the hen's is orangish with a black blotch.

Mallards belong to a group called puddle ducks, because they spend most of their time in shallow water. They feed by tipping over head-first, with their tail stuck straight up in the air while they eat aquatic plants, seeds, roots and invertebrates on the bottom. When frightened they can jump straight up into the air, unlike geese, which must run along the surface of the water to take off.

In the wild, mallards build a mounded nest of dead vegetation, hidden in tall grass or bushes near the water's edge. They are very comfortable around people, though, and near parks and rivers they often nest in flowerbeds and beneath shrubs in backyards. The 8–15 eggs hatch in three or four weeks, and the ducklings are immediately led off to water. The hen takes full charge of the nesting and chick-rearing, since the drake always deserts her once the eggs are laid.

Because they adapt well to people, mallards thrive around farms, housing developments and even in cities – wherever there is water and food. In some parks mallards can become so numerous that their droppings foul the water and they become a nuisance.

SPOTTER'S NOTES
- **Plumage** – Males: Green head, white neck ring, chestnut breast, gray body. Females: Mottled brown overall. Both have blue wing patches.
- **Size** – 23 in (57 cms) long.
- **Behavior** – Rambunctious flocks, with much squabbling and fighting.
- **Habitat** – Anywhere near bodies of water.

I D E N T I F I C A T I O N

- **Call**– Nasal *quaaack*.
- **Food** – Seeds, grass, aquatic plants, invertebrates, acorns, grain.
- **Nest** – Hidden on ground; mound of vegetation lined with down.
- **Eggs** – 8–15; off-white.

You may spot mallards that look strange, with odd color combinations, very large bodies or even feather tufts on their heads. These are hybrids between true mallards and domesticated duck varieties like Muscovies.

Wood Duck
AIX SPONSA

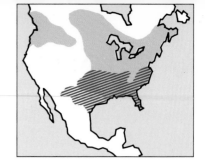

The wood duck is usually called North America's prettiest waterbird – and with good reason. The drake is beautifully colored in a rainbow of hues, and even the grayer hen is elegant.

"Woodies," as they are known, are primarily an eastern species, found from southern Canada to the Gulf of Mexico, and in scattered areas of the West. Smaller than a mallard, with a longer tail, they prefer streams, rivers and ponds deep in the forest, where they can feed on invertebrates, acorns and seeds that have fallen into the water.

The drake has a bright green head with a long crest; the throat is white, and the bird's beak and eye are bright red. The chest is maroon, the flanks pale yellow and his back blue. The gray hen also has a crest, and a white eye-stripe, but none of her mate's brilliant colors. Both sexes do have a blue speculum, though.

In keeping with where they live, wood ducks nest in hollow trees. The female picks a hole far above the ground, and lays up to 15 eggs in the cavity. The newly-hatched ducklings cannot fly, of course, but within 24 hours after they leave the egg, urged on by the hen, they jump, one by one, from the hole. They may drop 50 ft (15 m) or more, bouncing when they hit the ground, but they are so small and light that they are not hurt by the fall.

Wood ducks were once very rare, but today they are one of the most common ducks in the Northeast, although they are much shier around people than are mallards, and harder to find. They respond well to artificial nesting boxes, however, and building such boxes is a good way to increase the wood ducks in your area. Most conservation agencies distribute plans for nest boxes, which should be erected on tree trunks near streams, wooded swamps and small lakes.

When alarmed the wood duck does not quack, but instead gives a shrill, rising call: *ooo-eeek*.

SPOTTER'S NOTES

●● **Plumage** – Male: Green, crested head, maroon chest, yellowish flanks.
Females: Grayer, but with distinctive crest and long tail.
●● **Size** – Smaller than mallard; about 18 in (45cms) long.
●● **Behavior** – Secretive. Often seen flying in flocks at sunset.

IDENTIFICATION

●● **Call** – Shril, rising *ooo-eeek* given by hen.
●● **Food** – Acorns, seeds, insects.
●● **Nest** – Hollow tree as much as 50 ft (15m) above ground, lined with down.
●● **Eggs** – Up to 15; unmarked white.

Killdeer
CHARADRIUS VOCIFERUS

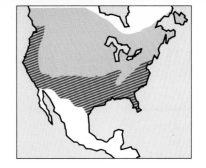

A shorebird that doesn't always live along the shore, the killdeer is a common bird in farm pastures, meadows, golf courses, open parks and along waterways. It is usually heard before it is seen, because its loud *kill-deeer!* call carries a long way.

A robin-sized bird with long legs and a short bill, the killdeer has a brown back, white undersides and two black bands across the throat and chest. Surprisingly, these bold markings actually make the killdeer harder to see, because they break up its outline, just as a tiger's stripes break up its form. The male and female are identical.

The killdeer's eggs are even better camouflaged – as they have to be, since the female builds no nest, but simply lays them on the ground, in a small depression in rocky soil or gravel. The four eggs are grayish-brown, covered with blackish spots and scrawls, and are very difficult to see. If an intruder (including a human) comes too close to the nest, the female killdeer puts on a convincing act, pretending that she has a broken wing and cannot fly. This lures the predator away from the nest – and once she thinks her eggs are safe, the killdeer suddenly "recovers" and flies off.

When the chicks hatch they are covered with brown, gray and white down that also conceals them. They leave the nest soon after they hatch, following their parents. When either adult gives a warning call, the chicks crouch low and freeze, trusting their very effective camouflage.

Killdeer often nest near people, laying their eggs along railroad tracks, in gravel quarries and anywhere else they can find stony soil. One pair in Pennsylvania nested for several years in a row on the flat roof of an elementary school. The chicks could not fly, however, and were trapped without food until the custodians caught them, put them in a bucket and lowered them to the ground, where their parents found them again.

SPOTTER'S NOTES

● **Plumage** – Sexes identical. Brown back, white undersides, two blacks bands on chest.
● **Size** – About 10 in (25cm) long.
● **Behavior** – Spends most of its time in open ground. Moves by running in short spurts.

I D E N T I F I C A T I O N

● **Call** – Drawn out *kill-deer*.
● **Food** – Insects, some seeds.
● **Nest** – None; eggs laid in depression in rocky soil.
● **Eggs** – Four, grayish with back spots and blotches.

Insects make up most of a killdeer's diet, although they do eat some weed seeds. In the summer killdeer are found over most of North America, but those in the North migrate to warmer climates for the winter. A few stay north through the cold weather, though, living along springs and streams that do not freeze.

Herring Gull
LARUS ARGENTATUS

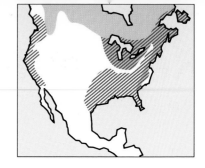

It is wrong to speak of "seagulls", since many kinds of gulls also live far from the sea. The The herring gull is one of these.
While it is common along both coasts, it can also be found on freshwater on the Great Lakes, in New England ponds and across much of Canada and Alaska.

Gulls can be difficult to tell apart, even for experts. Part of the problem is that it takes them three or four years to get their adult plumage. The herring gull, for example, starts out a solid, sooty brown with a brown bill. By its second winter it is lighter gray, with a light bill that has a dark tip. By the third winter the young herring gull has gray wings, and brown spots on its back and sides. The following spring it finally molts into its adult plumage – white head and body, pale gray wings with black tips, pink legs and a yellow bill with a red spot.

Herring gulls are scavengers, feeding on a wide variety of foods, depending on where they live. They will eat garbage, fish, clams and mussels (which they drop from the air on to roads to crack them open), berries, mice, reptiles and amphibians, bird eggs and chicks. Almost wiped out by market hunters at the turn of the century, herring gulls are very common today, thanks in large part to human dumps and landfills, which have allowed them to expand their range, as well. In fact, herring gulls are threatening rarer seabirds like roseate terns, because they prey on the terns' nests.

The herring gull's own nest is usually part of a larger colony on an offshore island. The nest is a simple cup of grasses, built on the ground and often lined with feathers. The eggs generally number three, and are buffy with darker brown spots. The chicks are covered with gray down at hatching, and as soon as they can leave the nest they form "creches" – groups of chicks, something like a nursery for birds. Even after they learn to fly the youngsters are fed by their parents for another five weeks, while they develop their hunting skills and coordination. When a chick is hungry it pecks at the red spot on its parent's bill, and the adult responds by regurgitating food.

SPOTTER'S NOTES
●● **Plumage** – Juvenile: Sooty brown overall; lightens over next three years. Adult: White head and body, gray wings with black tips, pink legs, yellow bill with red spots.
●● **Size** – About 25 in (62cms) long.
●● **Behavior** – Forms large, noisy flocks, especially around fishing boats or other food source. Bold and aggressive.
●● **Habitat** – Near large bodies of water, either fresh or salt.

IDENTIFICATION
●● **Call** – Loud *kee-yow, kee-yow, kee-yow.*
●● **Food** – Virtually anything caught, killed or scavenged.
●● **Nest** – Grass cup on ground, often part of larger colony
●● **Eggs** – 2-3; buffy with darker spots.

Red-tailed Hawk
BUTEO JAMAICENSIS

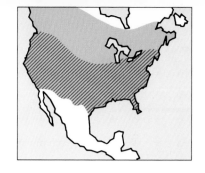

Some hawks shy away from people, staying in remote forests. Not so the red-tailed hawk, a common sight over woods and farmland throughout much of the continent.

The red-tail is a *buteo*, or soaring hawk. It has wide wings and a broad, fan-shaped tail, which help the hawk catch rising columns of sun-warmed air called thermals. Once in a thermal, the hawk can circle effortlessly as its scans the ground below for prey.

Red-tailed hawks don't have red tails, any more than robins have red breasts. The color is more a rusty orange, and is only visible when seen from above; from below – which is the perspective people usually see a hawk from – the tail looks pinkish. A better field mark is the red-tail's dark, streaky belly band, and the patch of black at the leading (or front) edge of each wing.

High in the air, a red-tail watches the ground carefully for movement, sometimes hovering in one place as it studies the cover below. If it sees a mouse, snake, rabbit or some other small animal, the hawk drops into what falconers call a "stoop," or dive, plummeting with folded wings. The hawk may exceed 100 mph as it stoops, braking at the last moment with its wings and tail, and grabbing its prey with powerful, clawed feet.

Red-tails frequently hunt over open country, but they usually nest along the edge of a forest or woodlot, high up in a large tree. The nest is a bulky platform of sticks, and may be used year after year; the pair also usually stay together for life. Two chicks is the normal number, although one or three are not uncommon. The babies are born downy and helpless, but grow quickly, and within five weeks or so have left the nest. Their parents care for them for about another month.

Mice and other small mammals make up most of a red-tail's food, but they also take some birds, reptiles, amphibians and large insects like grasshoppers.

SPOTTER'S NOTES

●● **Plumage** – Adult: Brown above, white below with dark with dark belly band, orangish tail. Immature: Similar, but tail brown with many small, dark bands.

●● **Size** – 20-25 in (50-62cms) long; females larger than males. Wingspan 48-52 in (120-130cms).

●● **Behavior** – Soars over open country hunting for food; often seen perched in dead trees near fields or roads.

●● **Habitat** – Mixture of woodlands and fields.

IDENTIFICATION

●● **Call**– High, descending scream: *ke-eeeee-rrr*.

●● **Food** – Mice, rabbits, rats, other small animals.

●● **Nest** – Platform of sticks high in tree, usually at edge of field.

●● **Eggs** – Usually 2; white with brown spotting.

Ring-necked Pheasant

PHASIANUS COLCHICUS

The ring-necked pheasant is so much a part of the country scene in the northern and western states that it is hard to believe that this multicolored bird isn't a native North American. Introduced from the Orient in the 1800s, it quickly established itself, especially in grain-farming regions like the Dakotas and upper Midwest.

The male ring-neck is unmistakable, with his long, pointed tail, green head, red eyepatch and maroon breast. The smaller hen is mottled brown, with a shorter tail, and can be mistaken for a sharp-tailed grouse or prairie chicken.

In the springtime, male ring-necks stake out courting territories, loudly proclaiming their ownership with noisy cackles, accompanied by drumming their wings in the air. A single male may assemble a group of a dozen or more hens, which he watches over and mates with. He takes no part in nesting, however; the hens go off individually and build their own nests, grass bowls hidden in hayfields and overgrown pastures. Clutches of eggs are large, with up to 15 eggs not being unusual. Many of the nests are destroyed (and the incubating females killed) by mowing machines cutting the hay, and for this reason ring-necked pheasants are becoming scarce in some areas.

Pheasants are grain and seed eaters for the most part, although insects are an important food in the summer. Young chicks eat almost nothing but insects, and on farms that are heavily sprayed with pesticides, the chicks may starve.

Ring-necks are fast fliers, but they prefer to run or hide to avoid danger. A male, despite his bright colors, can seemingly disappear into the background whenever he wants. When cut off from retreat a pheasant will flush — usually startling the person with its loudly flapping wings and harsh alarm cackle.

SPOTTER'S NOTES

●● **Plumage** – Male: Green head, white neck ring, bronze chest, long tail. Female: Shorter tail, brown mottling overall.

●● **Size** – Male, 33 in (82cms); female 20 in (50cms).

●● **Behavior** – Stays close to thick cover, flushing explosively if approached too closely. Male cackles in spring.

●● **Habitat** – Grain and hayfields, fencerows, cattail swamps (in winter).

IDENTIFICATION

●● **Call** – Male cackles to attract mate; both sexes also give alarm cackle when flushed.

●● **Food** – Grain, seeds, insects.

●● **Nest** – Grass bowl hidden in hay or tall grass.

●● **Eggs** – 7-15; unmarked buffy.

Bobwhite
COLINUS VIRGINIANUS

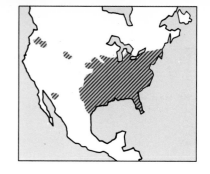

Small and plump, the bobwhite is the familiar qual of the East, Midwest and South, where it inhabits farmland, pine woods and suburban neighborhoods.

The quail gets its name from the male's springtime whistle, a rising *bob-WHITE*. Both sexes are rusty-brown, but the male has a small crest, and white throat and eye stripe that are buffy in the female. The bobwhite's tail is short, and its wings are rounded for short bursts of speed.

Living in flocks called coveys, the quail is a ground-dweller, picking its way through fields and briar tangles as it hunts for weed seeds, grain, foliage and insects. At night the covey, which may number 30 or 40 birds, sleeps in a tight circle with

their tails pointing inward and their heads facing out; in the event of danger, the covey will break in a dozen different directions, confusing the predator. Later, when trouble is past, they will give a quiet assembly call and rejoin each other.

The covey breaks up for the spring, when the females go off alone to nest. Each builds a shallow bowl of woven grass on the ground, often with an arch over the top to conceal the eggs from above. For further protection, the nest is often built in the middle of a thick clump of grass. There may be as many as 20 eggs, and some nests have been found with more than 40 eggs inside, suggesting that two females laid their eggs in the same nest. Like baby pheasants, the quail chicks can move and feed themselves within a few hours of hatching, and will follow their mothers for the next several weeks, learning the best places to eat, hide and drink. When they are about a month old, the chicks will join the coveys.

Bobwhite are found as far north as New England and the Great Lakes states, but they are not hardy in cold weather, and severe winters may kill many; combined with changes in farming methods has caused a decline in bobwhite.

IDENTIFICATION

- **Call** – Male whistles *bob-WHITE* in spring.
- **Food** – Grain, seeds, insects, leaves.
- **Nest** – Woven grass bowl on ground, often with arch over the top.
- **Eggs** – 6-20; white, often very pointed at one end.

SPOTTER'S NOTES

- **Plumage** – Reddish-brown mottling; male has white eye-stripe and throat, buffy in female.
- **Size** – About 10 in (25cms) long, plump.
- **Behavior** – Stays in flocks (coveys) near escape cover.
- **Habitat** – Farmlands, open woods, well-planted residential neighbourhoods.

Mourning Dove

ZENAIDA MACROURA

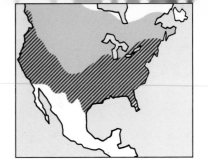

One of the most common birds in North America – and becoming more common every year – the mourning dove is found almost everywhere there are open spaces.

A little larger than a robin, the mourning dove is named for its somber call, a low *who-ooo-whoo-whoo-whoo*. It is not a flashy bird; both sexes are brownish-gray, with a touch of pinkish on the breast. The tail is long and pointed, and when the dove flares for a landing, you can see white and black edges to each feather. Young doves look similar, but often have a "scaly" appearance caused by dark feather edges, especially on the wings.

Mourning doves are very much at home with people, nesting in shade trees and coming eagerly to bird feeding stations. They are especially fond of cracked corn and white millet, but these birds are uncomfortable at raised feeders, so scatter the food on the ground. They also come to bird baths to drink, especially in the winter time, when the bath should be filled with warm water each morning.

Doves start nesting very early in the spring, often before migratory birds have even returned from the south. The male helps collect the twigs from which the nest is built, but the females does all the construction. The nest, built on a tree branch, is very frail looking (you can often see the eggs through the bottom), but it seems to hold together except in the strongest winds. There are usually just two eggs, but the doves will raise as many as six broods of chicks through the spring, summer and fall.

The babies get a very special meal for the first three or four days of life – "pigeon milk." It isn't really a milk, but a secretion from the crop of the parents (the crop is a part of the throat that stores grain when the dove eats). By the time the chicks are 7 or 8 days old, they are being fed on seeds and grain.

IDENTIFICATION

- **Song** – Low, mournful coos.
- **Food** – Grain, weed seeds.
- **Nest** – Loosely built twig platform in branches of trees.
- **Eggs** – 2; white.

SPOTTER'S NOTES

- **Plumage** – Plain grayish brown, long tail edged in white. Male has tiny patch of iridescent purple on neck.
- **Size** – About 10 in (30cms).
- **Behavior** – Flies rapidly in small flocks. Large groups often roost at night in pine trees.
- **Habitat** – Farmlands, deserts, suburbs, towns, city parks.

Rock Dove
COLUMBA LIVIA

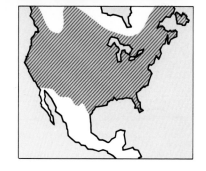

Better known as the pigeon, the rock dove was originally a wild bird in Europe and the Mediterranean, but was domesticated by man thousands of years ago. When the first settlers came to North America they brought captive pigeons with them, to be kept in outdoor "dove cotes" for their meat. Some inevitably escaped and formed wild colonies. Today they are most common around city skyscrapers, bridges and barns — habitat very similar to the cliffs where the original wild rock doves lived in Europe.

Most rock doves are bluish-gray, with a dark head and chest and light rump. There are many variations, though, ranging from pure white and solid black through rust, brown pale gray and an infinite combination of splotches. In flight they look big, with pointed wings and swift, direct flight — the reason domestic pigeons were used as message-carriers for many years.

Pigeons breed throughout the warm months, building a simple layer of grass or sticks on building ledges, under bridges, on the eaves of barns and silos. Two eggs are usually laid, with the male and female sharing the incubation duties through the 2½-weeks it takes the eggs to hatch. The chicks (called squabs) are fed on pigeon milk for their first few days, then a mix of milk and regurgitated grain, and finally just grain. By the time the squabs leave the nest they look very much like their parents — leading some city dwellers to wonder why they never see any baby pigeons.

Rock doves enliven the city landscape, but they can cause problems for people. Their droppings accumulate on building ledges and cornices, and the acid in them will eat away at the stone, destroying the beauty of the buildings. In a barn, the droppings can ruin hay or grain stored below.

SPOTTER'S NOTES
Plumage – Highly variable; usually bluish-gray.
Size – About 12 in (30cms), stocky body.
Behavior – Very tame around people. Fast, direct flight in tight flock.
Habitat – Cities, farms, suburbs, parks.

IDENTIFICATION

Call – Low coo.
Food – Weed seeds, corn, handouts.
Nest – Grass, straw or twig dish.
Eggs – 2; glossy white.

Great Horned Owl
BUBO VIRGINIANUS

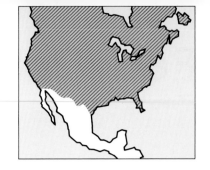

Great horned owls rule the night. No other owl is as heavy, as powerful and as bold as this magnificent nighttime hunter, flying through the darkness on wings that may stretch 5 ft (1½ m) from tip to tip.

No other owl is found over so wide an area – from the arctic to the southern tip of South America – and in as many different habitats. Great horned owls may be found in deep woodlands, farm country, deserts and tundra; they are common in tree-filled residential neighborhoods, and have been seen hunting for rats on deserted city streets.

By day, a great horned owl is difficult to spot, roosting quietly in a tree. The owl's plumage is a mix of brown, buff, white and black that breaks up its outline. The tufts of feathers that look like ears, or horns, have nothing to do with hearing, but simply help camouflage the owl even more by making it look like part of the tree. The owl's true ears are holes in the side of its head, hidden under the feathers of its round facial disc.

Great horned owls are the first bird to breed in the spring. The pairs (which stay together for many years, perhaps for life) begin calling to each other in January across most of the northern states, and by February or early March, have taken over an old crow or hawk nest and laid one to three eggs. The owlets hatch in about a month, covered in a thick coat of down to protect them from the cold. The parents guard them fiercely, even if they jump out of the nest.

A great horned owl will eat almost any small animal. Mice, rats, rabbits, shrews, opossums, skunks, birds, snakes, lizards, frogs, insects and even fish are taken. The owl uses its sharp claws and strong feet to kill its prey, which is eaten whole or in large chunks. Several hours later, the owl regurgitates a pellet composed of fur and bones, from which its meal can be determined.

SPOTTER'S NOTES
● ● **Plumage** – Mix of brown, buff, white and black two erect feather tufts look like ears. Yellow eyes, reddish-brown facial disc.

● ● **Size** – 20-25 in (50-62cms) long. Largest owl in most areas.

● ● **Behavior** – Hunts at night, roosts by day. Often harassed by flocks of crows.

● ● **Habitat** – Almost anywhere there are trees.

I D E N T I F I C A T I O N
● ● **Call** – Series of seven or eight deep hoots.

● ● **Food** – Almost any small animal or bird.

● ● **Nest** – Takes over abandoned bird or squirrel nest.

● ● **Eggs** – Usually 2; white, very round.

Eastern and Western Screech-owl

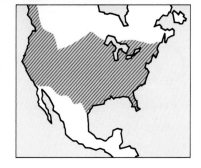

OTUS ASIO and OTUS KENNICOTTI

Often mistaken for a young great horned owl, the screech-owl has the same chunky body and erect ear tufts, but only grows 8 or 9 in (20-22cms) long.

There are two species – the eastern screech-owl, found from the Plains states east, and the western screech-owl in the mountains and Pacific coast states. They are almost identical, except for their calls; the eastern has a descending whistle that sounds like the whinny of a horse, while the western gives a series of short whistles that picks up tempo as it goes.

Eastern screech-owls come in two color phases: reddish-brown and gray. The phases have nothing to do with age or sex, although reddish birds are more common in the south and gray birds in the north. Western screech-owls are gray. All have yellow eyes and streaky, mottled plumage for camouflage, as well as a line of white spots on the back above the wings.

Because screech-owls are so small, it is not surprising that they take small prey, too. In the summer, large insects like grasshoppers, katydids, moths and crickets make up most of their diet, while in winter they take primarily mice and some songbirds. Like all owls, the screech-owl has special adaptations to the darkness. Their eyes are sensitive to light so they can see after sunset, and their wing feathers have special soft edges to muffle the sound of their flapping. Their hearing is excellent, and they have eight very sharp claws, called talons, for killing their prey.

Screech-owls nest in tree cavities, especially old woodpecker holes. Such natural cavities are scarce, however, and screech-owls are happy to accept a manmade substitute in the form of a large nest-box. The female usually lays four or five eggs, then incubates full-time while her mate catches food and brings it to her.

SPOTTER'S NOTES

●● **Plumage** – Two color phases in East, reddish-brown and gray; western birds all gray.

●● **Size** – Small; about 9 in (22cms) tall.

●● **Behavior** – Hunts at night. Often hunts along roads, and is hit by cars.

●● **Habitat** – Woodland, wooded parks, residential areas with old trees.

I D E N T I F I C A T I O N

●● **Call** – Eastern, descending whistle like horse whinny; western, series of short whistles or short trill, then long trill.

●● **Food** – Large insects, mice, small birds.

●● **Nest** – Tree cavity or large bird box.

●● **Eggs** – Usually 4 or 5; white round.

Common Nighthawk
CHORDEILES MINOR

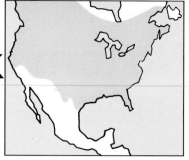

Cities are not good habitat for many birds, but the common nighthawk is one of the few that have adapted to the urban landscape.

Nighthawks are not hawks at all, but are members of an insect-eating group called nightjars, which includes the whip-poor-will. The nightjars swoop through the air snatching up bugs, an activity called "hawking" – hence the name. Nighthawks can often be seen at dusk, flying high above cities and towns. Their wings are long and pointed, with a white bar near the end of each wing; their tails are short and forked, and their flight is bouncy and mothlike.

Cities lure nighthawks because of the flat, gravel-covered rooftops of the buildings. Originally, nighthawks nested on rocky riverbanks, sandy or gravelly areas (and in some more remote places they still do), but many nighthawks now live in the city. The nest is nothing more than a shallow depression in the gravel, in which two eggs are laid. The female's problem is not keeping the eggs warm, but keeping them cool, because it can become blisteringly hot on the roof of building in summer – sometimes as high as 140 F degrees (60 C). The female shelters the eggs beneath her body, panting rapidly to get rid of excess body heat.

Nighthawks eat insects that they catch on the wing. A nighthawk's bill is very tiny, but when opened, the mouth is an enormous funnel for swallowing flies, beetles and moths. Most of the time the nighthawk is silent, except for mechanic *peent* calls, but during the nesting season the male performs a spectacular aerial display. Climbing high in the air, he rolls over into a dive toward his mate. As he falls, air rushing over special wing feathers makes a loud booming sound that carries through the night.

SPOTTER'S NOTES

● **Plumage** – Finely mottled gray and brown above, white below with fine black barring. One large white band on each wing.

● **Size** – 9-10 in (22-25 cms).

● **Behavior** – Hunts at night, especially twilight. Roosts during day

● **Habitat** – Common in cities; also in open country and sparse woods.

IDENTIFICATION

● **Call** – Nasal *peent;* also 'booming' display by male

● **Food** – Insects caught on the wing.

● **Nest** – None; depression in gravel.

● **Eggs** – 2; buff with fine brown speckles.

Northern Flicker
COLAPTES AURATUS

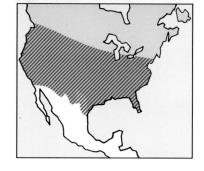

A woodpecker that spends a lot of time on the ground, the northern flicker is lured from the trees by its taste for ants, a favorite food. It is not unusual to see a flicker sitting near an anthill, using its barbed, sticky tongue to lap them up.

There are three color phases, which for years were considered separate species. The "yellow-shafted" form lives in the East; it has yellow wing linings and black mustache marks (present only in males). The "red-shafted" form is found from the Rockies west, and has a red mustache, while the "gilded" flicker of the Southwest combines yellow shafts and red mustaches.

A flicker is a large woodpecker, about the size of a mourning dove. Like all woodpeckers it has a thick, chisel-shaped bill that allows it to easily cut through wood, exposing the insects hidden inside. Its feet have strong claws for gripping tree trunks, and its tail feathers are very stiff, and are used as a brace when the flicker is climbing. In flight, this bird is easy to identify because it shows a large white rump patch, and flies with a distinct rising-and-falling pattern common to woodpeckers. The back is brown, the breast is buffy with black spots, and "yellow-shafted" flickers also have a crescent of bright red on the nape of the neck.

In spring the flickers chop a nest hole high in a tree, and lay a clutch of a half-dozen or so eggs. In many areas flickers are declining, in part because European starlings chase them out of their nest holes. One solution is to build special flicker nest-boxes, which are packed full of sawdust that the birds like to remove.

SPOTTER'S NOTES

●● **Plumage** – Brown back, spotted breast, white rump patch. Wing linings yellow in East and Southwest, red in west.

●● **Size** – 9-13 in (30-325 cms).

●● **Behavior** – Conspicious, noisy. Often flies across open fields

●● **Habitat** – Open woodlands, parks suburban neighbourhoods.

I D E N T I F I C A T I O N

●● **Call** – Loud *wik-up, wik-up, wik-up.*

●● **Food** – Insects, especially ants.

●● **Nest** – Chops nest hole high in tree.

●● **Eggs** – 5-8; pure white.

Downy Woodpecker
PICOIDES PUBESCENS

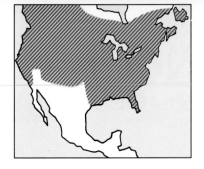

The smallest woodpecker in North America, the downy woodpecker is also one of the most common, found from the northern forests to Florida and California, and absent only from the extreme Southwest.

Less than 7 in (17 cms) long, the downy woodpecker moves like a wind-up toy, with nervous, jerky motions. It never seems to sit still for more than a moment or two as it hunts for insects or watches for danger. If it sees something it doesn't like, it gives a sharp *pik!* alarm call to alert anything that might be listening.

Males and females are similar — white below and black above, with white patches on the face, back and wings. Males have a small spot of crimson on the back of the head. The bill is very short and stubby — one way of telling the downy from its larger cousin the hairy woodpecker, which has a much longer beak.

Downy woodpeckers are woods dwellers, usually found in young hardwood forests, parks and tree-lined towns. They spend their time patiently working their way up tree limbs and trunks, looking for insects hidden in the cracks, or chopping away at dead wood to find the bugs underneath. Interestingly, males tend to hunt higher up in trees, and farther out on smaller branches, than do the females. Downies also eat seeds, berries (including poison ivy berries, which are poisonous for humans) and some fruit. Downy woodpeckers readily come to bird feeders for sunflower seeds and suet.

The nest hole is chopped by both sexes in a tree, often on the underside of a branch. Four or five eggs are normally laid.

SPOTTER'S NOTES

●● **Plumage** – Black-and-white, with white spotting on wings. Male has red patch on head.
●● **Size** – 6¾ in (16 cms).
●● **Behavior** – Nervous; stays in trees on trunk or limbs.
●● **Habitat** – Forests, parks, tree-lined neighbourhoods.

I D E N T I F I C A T I O N

●● **Call** – *Pik!* alarm note, also shrill whinny. Male drums rapidly on hollow wood in spring to attract female.

●● **Food** – Insects, seeds, berries.

●● **Nest** – Hole cut in tree or branch.

●● **Eggs** – 4-8; pure white.

Eastern Kingbird
TYRANNUS TYRANNUS

Eastern in name only, the eastern kingbird can be found as far west as Texas, Oregon and British Columbia, filling the summer air with its buzzy *dzeet-dzeet-dzeet-dzeet* calls.

A medium-sized songbird, the kingbird is a member of the flycatcher family, known for their quick, agile flights while catching insects. Its royal name comes from the kingbird's rough-and-tumble personality, chasing away intruding birds of many species, including hawks.

The kingbird is a handsome bird. The sexes are identical – black above, white below, with a white band at the tip of the tail and a tiny patch of red on the crown that is usually hidden by surrounding feathers. In the air the kingbird often flies on stiff wings held low, giving twitters as it goes; the birds also perch on treetops, fenceposts and wires.

Kingbirds are common in orchards, fencerows, open woods, parks and around homes. They nest in shrubs or low trees, about 10 or 15 ft (3-5 m) above the ground. The nest is woven of weed stems, grass fibers, plant down and leaves, lined with plant down. There are usually four or five eggs, which are very attractive – white with purplish-brown scrawl marks.

The kingbird has long been accused of catching bees, and will occasionally take a honeybee.

SPOTTER'S NOTES
●● **Plumage** – Black upperparts, white below, with white tail tip. Red head patch usually hidden.
●● **Size** – 8-9 in (20-22 cms).

●● **Behavior** – Boldly chases other birds, perches in open near treetops, fenceposts, etc.
●● **Habitat** – Farmlands, orchards, suburbia, along streams and rivers.

IDENTIFICATION

●● **Call** – Buzzy *dzeet-dzeet-dzeet-dzeet*.
●● **Food** – Insects, some berries and fruit, especially in fall.
●● **Nest** – Bulky cup in low tree or shrub.
●● **Eggs** – 3-6; white with purplish-brown scrawls.

Eastern Phoebe
SAYORNIS PHOEBE

A gentle harbinger of spring, the eastern phoebe is among the first birds to arrive in the North after the winter ends – in fact, it often appears when there is still snow on the ground, and must subsist on shriveled berries until the weather warms enough for insects to emerge.

The phoebe is a rather drab bird in plumage, with a dark brown head and upperparts, and a grayish breast. Its long tail is constantly pumped up and down – a good field mark, even in poor light. The song is neither sweet nor complicated, a very simple *fee-bee*, with the emphasis on the first syllable. But because the phoebe so often nests near humans, it is a favorite of many people.

In the wild the nest is built on rock ledges, cave entrances or cliffs, but today the phoebe is much more likely to use a bridge abutment (especially over a small stream in the woods), a barn foundation or the eaves of a house. The nest is small and well-built, covered with moss on the outside and lined with feathers or fur that the adult phoebes glean from the surrounding land. The eggs are incubated for a little more than two weeks, and the chicks spend another 16 or so days in it before they finally fly off for the first time.

Phoebes, like kingbirds, are flycatchers, and they display their abilities all day long. They choose a hunting perch, usually an exposed branch near a clearing or over a stream or pond. When an insect happens by the phoebe flies out, twists in the air to catch the bug, then returns to its perch. Throughout the day, it may make hundreds of attacks, many unsuccessful.

IDENTIFICATION

- **Song** – Short, harsh *fee-bee*.
- **Food** – Insects, some berries.
- **Nest** – Nicely formed cup of grasses, covered with moss and lined with feathers, fur.
- **Eggs** – 5 or 6; white.

SPOTTER'S NOTES

- **Plumage** – Sexes identical; dark head, brown upperparts, grayish breast (yellowish in fall). Long tail constantly pumped.
- **Size** – 8 in (17 cms).
- **Behavior** – Flycatches from perch, often near water.
- **Habitat** – Woodlands (especially near water), parks, wooded neighborhoods.

Barn Swallow
HIRUNDO RUSTICA

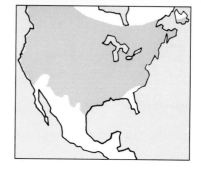

A flock of barn swallows, wheeling and diving over an open meadow, are such a part of summer in the country that it is hard to imagine a June day without them.

There are eight species of swallows in North America, but the barn swallow is certainly the best-known, in large part because it lives so close to human dwellings. Almost every barn and farm building has a few pairs that nest in its rafters, constructing their mud-and-grass nests in the shadows. This bird is absent, in fact, only from parts of the Deep South and of the desert Southwest.

An adult barn swallow is about about 7 in (17 cms) long, with delicate, pointed wings and a deeply forked tail. The upperparts are shiny, metallic blue, while the throat is reddish and the undersides cinnamon; young birds are grayer on the back, and paler beneath.

Barn swallows eat virtually nothing but insects, captured on the wing. They are superb fliers, able to make snap turns and rolls as they chase flying insects, sometimes skimming only inches above the ground. They even drink and bathe on the wing, dipping one wingtip into the water and rolling the drops across the back, or slicing the lower beak across the surface for a sip.

A barn swallow nest, built by both sexes, is mostly mud and straw; the birds collect small pellets of mud from nearby puddles, and use them to plaster hay, straw and grass together on a beam. The final touch is a lining of white poultry feathers.

SPOTTER'S NOTES

● ● **Plumage** – Shiny dark blue upperparts, buffy belly, reddish-brown throat. Forked tail.

● ● **Size** – About 7 in.

● ● **Behavior** – Acrobatic flights over open fields, singly or in flocks.

● ● **Habitat** – Farmland, fields, open areas.

I D E N T I F I C A T I O N

● ● **Call** – Rapid twitter.

● ● **Food** – Insects, taken on the wing.

● ● **Nest** – Mud and straw, lined with feathers.

● ● **Eggs** – 4-5; white, spotted with brown.

Blue Jay
CYANOCITTA CRISTATA

The sentinel of the woods, the blue jay lets the whole world know if it sees something amiss: *Jay! Jay! Jay!* goes its loud alarm cry, alerting other birds and animals of danger.

As pretty as it is loud, the blue jay has cobalt-blue plumage, set off by pale gray underparts and white trim on the wingbars and tail, and a black breast band and eye-stripe. A cocky crest rises or falls on the bird's head at will. Its plumage and personality combine to make it a very noticeable bird wherever it lives.

Home for the blue jay are forests (especially oak and hickory woodlands), parks, suburban backyards and tree-lined streets, from the Great Plains east; the Stellar's jay, similar but with an all-black head, inhabits western forests. Except in the nesting season, the blue jay is a flock bird, traveling in bands of a dozen or more. They are intelligent and curious – and almost fearless. If a house cat or hawk should venture too close to a nest, it will be mercilessly dive-bombed by jays giving their shrill war-cry.

Blue jays are not picky about what they eat, and will take fruit, berries, acorns, seeds, insects, worms and small animals. They will also rob the nests of other songbirds, taking the eggs and small chicks – a fact that has sometimes angered people, who forget that in nature, one thing must die so another can live. In the web of life, a baby bird and a grasshopper are equally important.

Jays nest in the mid-level of tall trees, usually picking a conifer if they can. The nest is made of hundreds of twigs – the largest forming the base, with progressively smaller twigs, pieces of leaves and roots forming the inner cup. As with most songbirds the eggs usually number four or five. While they are caring for the eggs and chicks, the parents remain rather quiet, to hide the fact that they have a nest nearby.

I D E N T I F I C A T I O N

- **Call** – Loud, repeated *Jay!* Also a bell-like note, and a descending scream like a hawk's.
- **Food** – Wide variety of vegetable and animal foods, including young birds.
- **Nest** – Cup of twigs, leaves, grass, rootlets, usually in coniferous tree.
- **Eggs** – 3-6; olive with brown spots.

SPOTTER'S NOTES
- **Plumage** – Blue above, pale below, with black chest band and white on wings and tail. Crest on head.
- **Size** – About 11 in (27 cms).
- **Behavior** – Bold, noisy and curious. Usually seen in flocks.
- **Habitat** – Open woodlands, groves, parks.

Black-billed Magpie
PICA PICA

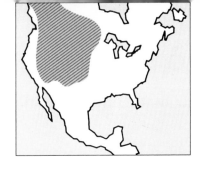

There is no mistaking a magpie – no other bird has that long tail and bold, black-and-white pattern. There are two species; the black-billed magpie is common over much of the West, while the very similar yellow-billed magpie is restricted to central California.

Magpies are members of the crow family, along with jays, and like crows and jays, they have a keen intelligence and boundless sense of curiosity. They are insect-hunters and scavengers, and find especially rich pickings after the winter snows melt, revealing the carcasses of elk, deer and moose that did not make it through through the cold. Magpies also eat some fruits and seeds, and aren't above filching scraps from a dumpster behind a fast-food restaurant.

Black-billed magpies inhabit open country and sparse woods, especially thickets along streams (called riparian habitat by scientists). Here they nest, building a monstrous collection of sticks and twigs formed into a sphere, with two side entrances and a lining of dried cow droppings. They lay six or seven eggs each year, adding new

SPOTTER'S NOTES
Plumage – Unmistakable; long tail, black-and-white plumage.
Size – Roughly 20 in (50 cms) long.
Behavior – Inquisitive. Often perches on fenceposts along roads.
Habitat – Open forests, rangeland, along streams.

I D E N T I F I C A T I O N
Call – *Mag* or *chek-chek-chek* notes.
Food – Insects; also scavenges.
Nest – Huge dome of sticks and twigs with side entrances.
Eggs – 6-7; greenish with fine brown spotting.

material each season to the remains of the previous year's nest. Magpies often breed in loose colonies, just as they often travel in small flocks.

The black-billed magpie is technically a songbird, but the best it can manage is a high-pitched *mag* call, and a series of *chek-chek-chek* notes.

American Crow
CORVUS BRACHYHYNCHOS

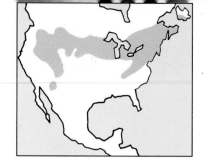

The crow is an easy bird for beginning bird-watchers to identify — it is the only large, all-black bird found in most places, and its loud *caw* call is also distinctive.

Crows are expert scavengers, eating whatever opportunity brings their way — road-killed animals, sprouting corn, frogs or small snakes, large insects, bird eggs or chicks, berries, fruit, mice and many other things. Except when they are nesting, American crows stay in flocks, and during the winter they may congregate in enormous roosts that hold hundreds of thousands of birds.

American crows are highly social birds. They communicate by voice, and have a wide "vocabulary" of caws, croaks and other noises — some alarm calls, some greetings, some assembly calls. When a crow spots a large hawk, like a red-tail, it gives a special warning call that attracts dozens of other crows, which mob together to drive the hawk away. Crows especially hate great horned owls (which hunt them at night while they are on roost), and may gather by the hundreds to harass an owl caught in the open in daylight.

A crow pair takes almost two weeks to build their large stick, twig and bark nest high in a tree. The eggs are very attractive — blue-green with a heavy coat of brown spots. The number of eggs ranges from three to eight, with five being a normal clutch.

There are two other species of crows in North America which look almost identical to the American crow. The fish crow, slightly smaller with a nasal *cah* call, is found in the Mississippi, and along the Southeast coast. The northwestern crow is found along the coasts of British Columbia and Alaska, and has a hoarse caw.

SPOTTER'S NOTES
●● **Plumage** — Glossy black.
●● **Size** — About 17 in (42 cms) long.
●● **Behavior** — Forms large flocks. Very wary, but often feeds along roads.
●● **Habitat** — Farmlands, woods, deserts, towns, city parks, seashores.

I D E N T I F I C A T I O N

●● **Call** — *Mag* or boisterous *caw!*
●● **Food** — Scavenger; eats virtually anything
●● **Nest** — Large, built of sticks, twigs, bark high in tree
●● **Eggs** — 3-8; bluish-green with brown spotting.

Black-capped Chickadee

PARUS ATRICAPILLUS

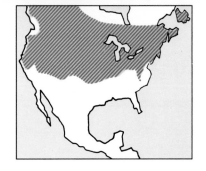

On a cold winter's day, a chickadee can seem like the friendliest bird in the woods, as it flits from branch to branch, spilling its whistled *chick-a-dee-dee-dee* calls as it goes. And if you purse your lips and squeak, or making a whispery "pishing" sound with your lips, the chickadee may even flit down within a few feet of you, to see what's making such a fuss.

Chickadees are small birds, just over 5 in (12 cms) long. They have a plump body, round head and fairly long tail, but their best field mark is the black cap and black throat – and the call, which the chickadee rarely stops whistling, although sometimes it cuts it down to just the *dee-dee-dee* part.

The black-capped chickadee, found across the northern half of the U.S. and most of Canada, is the most common of the seven chickadee species. The Carolina chickadee of the Southeast and Midwest looks very much like the black-capped, but has a higher, faster call. The mountain chickadee of the West has a white eyebrow, and the boreal chickadee of Canada and Alaska has a brown cap.

SPOTTER'S NOTES

●● **Plumage** –
Black cap and throat, gray body, peach on flanks in fall, winter. Sexes similar.

●● **Size** – About 5 in (12 cms) long.

●● **Behavior** –
Active and curious. Forms flocks in winter with titmice, kinglets, downy woodpeckers.

●● **Habitat** – Hardwood and mixed forests, groves, fencerows, wooded neighborhoods.

I D E N T I F I C A T I O N

●● **Call** – Whistled *chick-a-dee-dee-dee;* song is a whistled *fee-bee-bee*.

●● **Food** – Insects, seeds, berries, small fruit.

●● **Nest** – Hole cut in rotting tree or stump.

●● **Eggs** – 6-10; white with rusty speckles at large end.

All chickadees share the same curiosity and tameness, however. They come eagerly to bird feeders for sunflower seeds and suet, and with patience you can teach them to sit on your hand to take seeds. In the summer they feed largely on insects, while during the winter their diet includes hibernating spiders, seeds, berries and fruit.

Chickadees nest in dead trees and stumps, making a deep nest hole by tearing at the rotten wood with their beaks. They then line the hole with plant down, feathers and animal fur. If a racoon or other predator disturbs the nest while the female is incubating, she gives a loud hiss that sounds very much like a snake – and scares off the predator.

White-breasted Nuthatch

SITTA CAROLINENSIS

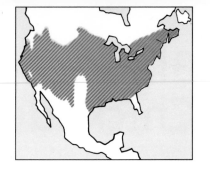

The white-breasted nuthatch goes through life looking at an upside-down world. Like a woodpecker, a nuthatch looks for insects on the trunks of trees, but it does so by climbing down the tree head-first. That way, it finds insects that other birds have missed.

Even though the nuthatch isn't related to woodpeckers, it has some of the same adaptations. Its feet have large, hooked claws for gripping the tree bark, and its bill is stout and sharp – not for hammering on dead wood like a woodpecker, but for prying away pieces of bark to expose hidden insects. When it is looking for food, a nuthatch flies to the top of a tree trunk, then works its way down, head-first, in a spiral, investigating every nook and cranny; then it flies to the top of the next tree and starts all over again. The nuthatch can also perch upright.

The odd name, nuthatch, apparently comes from an old English word, "nut-hack" – an accurate label, because nuthatches will feed on acorns that they hack into smaller pieces. They will also take seed, suet and peanut butter from a bird feeder.

IDENTIFICATION

- **Call** – Nasal *yank, yank, yank.*
- **Food** – Insects, spiders, seeds, berries, nuts.
- **Nest** – Natural cavity, woodpecker hole, birdbox.
- **Eggs** – 6-10; white with purplish spots.

SPOTTER'S NOTES

Plumage – Black cap, white breast, bluish back. Chestnut patch between legs. Female is duller and grayer than male.

Size – About 6 in (15 cms) long.

Behavior – Climbs down trees head-first.

Habitat – Forests, wooded neighbourhoods.

Oddly, for a bird with such a sharp bill, the nuthatch does not chop its own nest hole, but relies instead on natural cavities, birdboxes or old woodpecker holes. The adults will sometimes catch a beetle or ant and sweep the crushed bug around the entrance to the nest; because many insects release foul-smelling chemicals when captured, this may keep predators away.

House Wren
TROGLODYTES AEDON

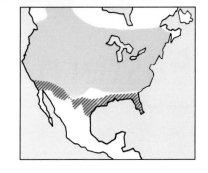

The bubbly song of the house wren fills gardens, thickets and backyards each spring, when these tiny, mousy birds return from their southern wintering grounds.

The house wren is a midget among birds, about 4¾ in (12 cms) long, but with an endless supply of energy. A male, staking out his territory, flits constantly from one perch to another, bursting with song, ready to tussle with a rival and chase him away. When angry, the wren cocks his tail straight up and lowers his head, bobbing from side to side while chattering excitedly.

While a house wren's song is lovely, its color is fairly drab – rusty brown above, buffy below, with dark barring on the sides, back and tail. Western and Southwestern birds are grayer than those in the East. The sexes are colored alike, and apparently males and females tell each other apart through voice and behavior.

House wrens will nest in almost any cavity they find – natural or manmade. They accept birdboxes without hesitation, but they have also been known to nest in drain pipes, empty tin cans, clothespin bags, the pockets of clothing hanging out to dry on a line, even the exhaust pipes of unused cars. Males will also build "dummy nests" in all the cavities within their territory, perhaps to keep other birds away, perhaps to fool predators.

SPOTTER'S NOTES

●● **Plumage** – Rusty brown above, buff below, with dark barring. Sexes similar.

●● **Size** – 4¾ in (12 cm) long.

●● **Behavior** – Curious, aggressive with other birds. Attract by squeaking.

●● **Habitat** – Backyards, thickets, fencrows.

IDENTIFICATION

●● **Song** – Bubbling, rolling series of short whistles.

●● **Food** – Insects, spiders.

●● **Nest** – Natural or manmade cavity.

●● **Eggs** – 5-8; white with heavy reddish-brown speckling.

Eastern Bluebird
SIALIA SIALIS

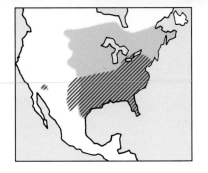

The bluebird was once almost as common in the East as the robin is today, until a combination of problems made this beautiful bird a rarity. Now, with human help, the eastern bluebird is again becoming an everyday sight along country roads and around homes.

A male bluebird is gorgeous – deep blue on the head, back and wings, chestnut-red on the throat and chest, and white on the belly. The female is duller but still very attractive. The male's song is a rich, musical warble, and he sings a snatch of it – *churl-lee* – as a call year-round.

Bluebirds are cavity-nesters, but they cannot make their own holes, so they depend on old woodpecker nests and natural cavities. In the 1800s, when every farm had miles of wooden fenceposts around the pastures, bluebirds had an abundance of nesting sites, but by the turn of the century two things happened. Farmers began to use metal fenceposts, and the English sparrow and European starling had been introduced to North America. Both of these alien species quickly chased the bluebirds out of the remaining nests, and suddenly the bluebird was a rare sight where it had once been so common.

Fortunately, bluebirds take well to manmade birdboxes, and the placement of thousands of bluebird boxes across the eastern U.S. and southern Canada – each with a hole big enough for a bluebird but not big enough to admit a starling – has given this pretty thrush a second chance. A bluebird box should be about 12 in (30 cms) deep, with a 1½-in (3.75 cms) entrance hole; place the box on a post about six ft (2 m) high, and face it to the south or east, away from the wind.

SPOTTER'S NOTES

- ●● **Plumage** – Deep blue above, reddish chest, white belly. Female duller. Juveniles have spotted gray breast, bluish wings.
- ●● **Size** – About 6 in (15 cms) long.
- ●● **Behavior** – May stay north in flocks during winter. Often perch on wires or in trees and fly to ground for insects.
- ●● **Habitat** – Orchards, meadows, fencerows, backyards.

IDENTIFICATION

- ●● **Song** – Rich warbler; call, whistled *churl-lee*.
- ●● **Food** – Insects, worms, fruit. In winter largely berries.
- ●● **Nest** – Often in birdboxes; also natural cavities, old woodpecker holes.
- ●● **Eggs** – 4 or 5; pale blue.

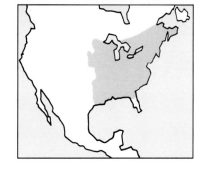

Wood Thrush
HYOCICHLA MUSTELINA

It is generally conceded that the wood thrush has one of the loveliest songs of any North American bird – perhaps the loveliest of all. It is heard most often at daybreak in the spring, when the trees are just bursting into leaf and the woods are silent. The song is long series of flute-like notes, angelic in their clarity, rising and falling, with dramatic pauses in between: *ee-o-LEE . . . EE-o-lay . . .ee-o-LEE.*

The male wood thrush usually picks a low perch from which to sing, a horizontal branch or bent sapling within 10 or 15 ft (3-4 m) of the ground. It sits quietly while singing, and may be difficult at first to spot. The sexes are identical, with brown upperparts, bright rufous on the head, and white breasts with sharp, round black spots. The similar hermit thrush has rufous on the tail, and less distinct breast spots.

Wood thrushes are found from New England to northern Florida and west to the edge of the Plains, extending into the prairies along wooded river valleys. They inhabit mixed or deciduous woods, especially those that are damp, such as in stream valleys. Within such habitats the female wood thrush picks a tree branch, usually close to the ground but occasionally as high as 50 ft (15 m), and builds a base of leaves and mud. On this foundation she constructs the cup using grass, moss, strips of fine bark and lined with rootlets. Most clutches number three or four eggs, which are a solid blue-green, not as intense as the color of a robin's egg.

The wood thrush eats insects and a great deal of small fruit. It winters in Central America and northern South America, which may put it at risk from tropical deforestation.

I D E N T I F I C A T I O N

●● **Song** – Lovely series of flute-like phrases
●● **Food** – Insects, fruit and berries.
●● **Nest** – On horizontal tree branch; always has foundation of leaves.
●● **Eggs** – 3–4; pale blue-green.

SPOTTER'S NOTES
●● **Plumage** – Brown upperparts, bright rufous on head; white breast with round, black spots. Sexes similar.
●● **Size** – About 7 in (15.5 cms).
●● **Behavior** – Sings very early, often before other birds.
●● **Habitat** – Nests in damp deciduous and mixed forests.

American Robin

TURDUS MIGRATORIUS

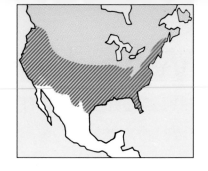

The robin is probably the best-known bird in North America. Just about everyone is familiar with its rusty orange breast and the way it patrols lawns for worms. But the robin is more than a suburban bird; it is found from the arctic tundra to the deserts, in swamps, on mountains, in forests and near the sea.

The robin is our largest thrush, about 10 in (25 cms) long (and is so well-known that bird-watchers often describe other birds as being "robin-sized"). Males have a dark head, brown back, wings and tail, and a deep brick-orange breast; females are duller, but both sexes have white corners on the tail. A young robin has an orangish breast covered with black spots.

While earthworms are certainly an important food for robins, they are not this species' sole diet, for robins take a wide variety of insects and invertebrates, as well as fruit and berries. When hunting for worms a robin will pause, cock its head to one side as if listening, then stab into the dirt for the worm. The robin is not listening, though – it is carefully watching the soil and the grass stems, which will move slightly if a worm is beneath them.

The robin's nest, built of grass and weed stems plastered together with mud, is a masterpiece of construction. It is often built in the crotch of a tree trunk or branch, but may also be placed on a porch beam, windowsill or electric meter box. A simple wooden platform about 8 in (20 cms) square, erected on a sheltered wall, will also attract nesting robins.

I D E N T I F I C A T I O N

- **Song** – Rolling *cheerily-cherryup-cheerio*; call a chuckling *chuck-chuck-chuck*.
- **Food** – Earthworms, insects, invertebrates, fruit, berries.
- **Nest** – Large, neat cup of grass and weed leaves cemented with mud.
- **Eggs** – 4-6; bluish-green.

SPOTTER'S NOTES

- **Plumage** – Brick-orange breast, dark head, brown upperparts; female duller. Juveniles have spotted breasts.
- **Size** – 10 in (25 cms).
- **Behavior** – Often fearless around people.
- **Habitat** – Almost anywhere, especially around homes.

Gray Catbird
DUMETELLA CAROLINENSIS

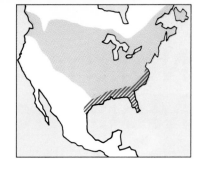

Something rustles deep in a thicket. There is a moment of silence, then a loud *Mew! Mew!* A cat? No, a catbird, which has a call that sounds very much like a kitten's cry. The catbird is also a skillful mimic, imitating the calls of many other birds, although it is not as good a mimic as its close relative, the northern mockingbird.

A catbird is sooty gray (males and females are colored alike) with a black cap and a patch of chestnut beneath its long tail. It is a bird of the thickets, living in brushy areas where brambles and young trees crowd close together — places like fencerows, overgrown fields and lush gardens. The catbird is a skulker, staying deep within cover, where it scolds intruders with nasal, drawn-out *mews*.

The nest is usually built within 10 ft (3 m) of the ground, in shrubs or small trees. Both the male and female work on it, collecting thick twigs and strips of bark (especially grapevine bark) for the base, then forming the cup from finer materials.

The eggs are blue-green, very much like a robin's, and hatch within two weeks. The male takes most of the responsibility for feeding the chicks, collecting insects all day long. Like many birds, adult catbirds eat a great deal of fruit and berries, but feed their young almost exclusively on insects, which are higher in protein.

During the breeding season, catbirds are found over most of the U.S. and southern Canada, except for the far West and Southwest. In winter they may migrate as far as Central America, although some winter along the Atlantic and Gulf coasts.

SPOTTER'S NOTES

●● **Plumage** – Sooty gray, with black cap and chestnut patch under tail.
●● **Size** – About 9 in (22 cms).
●● **Behavior** – Scolds intruders from thick cover. Responds well to squeaking.
●● **Habitat** – Thickets, overgrown fields, gardens.

IDENTIFICATION

●● **Call** – Mimics other birds, interspersed with cat-like *mew* calls.
●● **Food** – Insects, berries, fruit.
●● **Nest** – Built near ground in shrub or small tree; base of twigs and bark. Fairly large for size of bird.
●● **Eggs** – 4-5; greenish-blue.

Northern Mockingbird

MIMUS POLYGLOTTOS

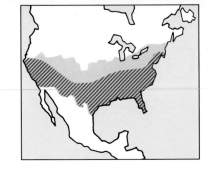

The mockingbird's reputation as a singer can hardly be overestimated. A male mocker (as they are often known) may sing snatches of more than 30 different bird songs in a 10-minute period, along with his own original tunes and such non-musical sounds as whistles and siren imitations.

There are several North American birds that mimic the songs of others, but the mockingbird is the champion of all; sometimes it is hard to tell if you are hearing the real song, or a mockingbird's imitation. However, the mocker has a short attention span, and usually only repeats a phrase three or four times before going on to something new. The mockingbird is also one of the only songbirds to sing at night, especially if the moon is full.

Northern mockingbirds are actually southern in their distribution (the "northern" in their name separates them from tropical species like the Bahama mockingbird), found from southern New England, Nebraska and northern California on south. In the past 30 years they have made an impressive push to the north, colonizing areas where they were never found before. Some experts believe people, by planting berry-producing bushes like multiflora rose and firethorn that provide the mockingbird with winter food, have made this possible.

The mockingbird is a fairly plain, gray bird, with dark wings and tail. In flight it shows highly visible "flash marks" of white on the wings, and white outer tail feathers. The beak is thin and slightly down-curved, and the eye is yellow. Young mockingbirds are browner, and have faint spots on the breast.

In the summer mockingbirds feed on insects, berries and fruit, switching to a higher percentage of berries in winter. Mockers sometimes come to bird feeders (they love raisins and cracked corn) but they are so territorial that they sometimes drive all the other birds away.

SPOTTER'S NOTES

Plumage – Pale gray, with dark wings and tail; white "flash marks" on wings and tail.

Size – About 10 in (22 cms).

Behavior – Conspicuous on lawns, TV antennae, bushes. Often flashes wings to scare up insects.

Habitat – Suburbs, towns, fencrows, thickets.

IDENTIFICATION

Call – Mimics other species (and non-bird sounds), usually repeating each phrase several times.

Food – Insects, berries, fruit.

Nest – Near ground in shrub or bush; prickly twig base, lined with brown rootlets.

Eggs – 4-5; bluish with large brown splotches

European Starling
STURNUS VULGARIS

Because of a small group's misguided love of literature, North America has the starling — an aggressive, bullying bird that has played a big role in the decline of such native species as the eastern bluebird and northern flicker.

In 1890, a group called the American Acclimatization Society released 60 starlings in New York City's Central Park, all because the bird is mentioned in one of Shakespeare's plays, and this group wanted "the birds of the Bard" to be found in the U.S. Within 60 years the starling was found across the entire continent, numbering in the billions.

Starlings are such a nuisance that it is easy to overlook their good points. They eat large numbers of Japanese beetle grubs (another introduced pest), and their breeding plumage, glossy green and purple, is rather attractive. Balancing that, however, are many bad points, the worst of which is the starling's habit of taking over nest cavities used by bluebirds, woodpeckers, tree swallows, purple martins and other native birds. For bluebirds, the solution is to erect bird boxes with an entrance hole too small for the starlings.

Unfortunately, that approach cannot be used for bigger birds like flickers.

Starlings are omnivorous, meaning that they eat a wide variety of plant and animal food, including insects, invertebrates, seeds, fruit, berries and human trash. They can be a pest at a bird feeder, hogging the food and keeping smaller, more desirable species away. The nest, in a cavity or hole, is a collection of leaves, paper, straw, grass and debris, holding four to six pale bluish eggs. The male's song creaks like a rusted hinge, although the starling can also mimic other birds. In the late summer through winter, starlings congregate in flocks that can number anywhere from a few dozen to several million.

SPOTTER'S NOTES

●● **Plumage** – Breeding season, black with glossy green and purple iridescence, yellow bill. Winter, black with white spots, black bill. Juvenile buffy brown.

●● **Size** – 8-9 in (22 cms).

●● **Behavior** – Usually seen in flocks, feeding on ground or trees.

●● **Habitat** – Cities, towns, suburbs, farms, Rarely found far from human habitation.

IDENTIFICATION

●● **Song** – Creaky notes and warbles; also mimics other birds.

●● **Food** – Wide variety of insects, fruit, berries, seeds.

●● **Nest** – In cavity; large collection of grass, weeds, trash.

●● **Eggs** – 4-6; pale bluish-white.

Red-eyed Vireo
VIREO OLIVACEOUS

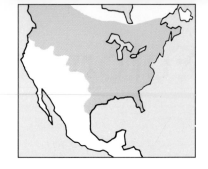

High in the treetops, a red-eyed vireo sings its song tirelessly. Long after the dawn chorus has stopped, and on through the midday when the forest is quiet, the vireo keeps up its tune, a never-ending string of brief phrases separated by short pauses. For this reason, the red-eyed vireo was once known as the "preacher bird," because it reminded people of a minister who wouldn't stop preaching.

At one time, the red-eyed vireo was considered the most common bird in the eastern hardwood forests – but no more. This bird spends the winter in the western Amazon rain forest of South America, and the destruction of the tropical forest has brought a decline in its numbers. There are problems in its North American range as well; vireos like unbroken forests, so as our woodlands are cut into smaller and smaller fragments it loses nesting habitat. Fragmentation also brings cowbirds into the forest, where they seek out songbird nests, throw out the eggs and lay their own instead.

The red-eyed vireo is a rather plain bird, with identical plumage for males and females. The breast is pale, the back dark olive and the cap gray, with a black-bordered white eyeline that is its best field mark (the red eye is actually very difficult to see). This species usually stays high in the treetops, hidden by leaves, so knowing its song is the best way to find it. Its range stretches from the East and Southeast through most of Canada.

Vireos are master builders, constructing a beautifully formed cup of grass, plant down and leaves, covered with spider webs and hung in the forked branch of a sapling 10 or 15 ft (3-4 m) above the ground. The vireo's eggs (so often supplanted by a cowbird's) are white, with fine brown spots at the large end.

SPOTTER'S NOTES
Plumage – Olive back, pale breast, blue-gray cap, black-bordered white eyeline. Sexes identical.
Size – About 6 in 15 cms).

Behavior – Tireless singer in spring. Stays high in treetops.
Habitat – Deciduous woodlands.

IDENTIFICATION

Song – Short phrases with brief pauses, repeated endlessly.
Food – Insects and spiders.
Nest – Cup of grass, leaves, plant down, spider webs, hung in forked branch.
Eggs – Usually 4; white with brown spots at large end.

Yellow-rumped Warbler

DENDROICA CORONATA

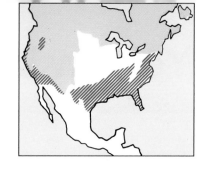

Bright splashes of yellow on the rump, sides and head make this bird one of the prettiest of the spring migrants — although, unlike most warblers, it may linger through winter in many areas, eating the berries of poison ivy or bayberry instead of its summer diet of insects.

In breeding plumage, the male is dark blue-gray, with white wingbars and belly; females are similar but browner. Birds in the East have a white throat, while western birds have yellow. Until a few years ago, these two forms were thought to be different species — the "myrtle" warbler in the East, and "Audubon's" warbler in the West. Closer study showed that they interbreed, so scientists now consider them one variety.

The nesting range of the yellow-rumped warbler runs from eastern Canada and New England to Alaska, and down over most of the West. It winters farther north than any other warbler, from the Midwest and Mid-Atlantic States (especially along the coast) to Texas and parts of the Southwest. In a few areas of the Pacific Northwest it is a year-round resident. Like most warblers, the yellow-rumped molts its

SPOTTER'S NOTES

Plumage — Breeding male, dark blue-gray with yellow on sides, rump, crown. Throat white in East yellow in West. Female and fall adults similar but browner.

Size — About 5½ in (14 cms).

Behavior — Forms large flocks in winter, staying close to berry sources.

Habitat — Nests in coniferous or mixed forests. In winter on coat, in tangles of poison ivy, bayberry, wax myrtle.

IDENTIFICATION

Song — Trill that may rise or drop at end.

Food — Insects in summer, berries in winter.

Nest — In conifer tree; many feathers woven into lining.

Eggs — 3-5; white with brown wreath at large end

feathers in early fall, taking on drabber colors for the winter. It can still be identified by the yellow on the rump and sides, however.

The nest, built on a flat spruce tree branch, uses many feathers as a lining, woven into the cup so the tops curl in, hiding the eggs.

Yellow Warbler
DENDROICA PETECHIA

Almost everywhere wet thickets are found, the rapid-fire song of the yellow warbler can be heard – *sweet sweet sweet I'm so sweet*, the bird seems to be saying. Watch for a moment, and you're sure to see the male, a speck of bright gold flitting from one treetop perch to another.

The yellow warbler is found over virtually all of the U.S. and Canada, except for the extreme South and Texas. The male is pure yellow, with somewhat darker wings and streaks of bright chestnut on his breast; the female is yellow below and greenish above, and lacks the breast streaks.

Willows are a favorite of the yellow warbler, especially young, bushy willows that crowd along the edge of a stream or river. The nest is built within 10 ft (3 m) of the ground, in an upright crotch in a sapling. The female collects plant down, reinforcing it with grass and weed stems, to form a deep, fluffy cup. She may also steal nesting material from a neighbor's nest, particularly where there are many yellow warblers breeding in a small area, as often happens. Should cowbirds lay their eggs in the warbler's nest, she may simply build another layer on top and try again.

Insects make up almost the entire diet of the yellow warbler – insects gleaned from the undersides of leaves, from cracks in bark, or caught in flight like a flycatcher. When the male is courting a female, he will bring her insects as a gift, which she accepts by begging like a chick.

SPOTTER'S NOTES

●● **Plumage** – Male bright yellow, with chestnut streaks on breast. Female and immature male similar but duller, without streaks.
●● **Size** – 5 in (12 cms).
●● **Behavior** – Lively, conspicuous. Males often chase each other through air.
●● **Habitat** – Thickets near streams, moist fields, swamps.

I D E N T I F I C A T I O N

●● **Song** – Rapid *sweet sweet sweet I'm so sweet*.
●● **Food** – Insects.
●● **Nest** – Built in upright crotch of sapling; largely of plant down.
●● **Eggs** – 4-5; white with pale brownish splotches.

Common Yellowthroat

GEOTHYLPIS TRICHAS

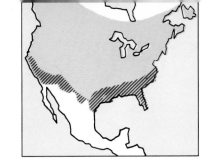

The yellowthroat is probably the most abundant warbler in North America, absent only from the arctic. Everywhere else — in thickets, marshes, fencerows, brushy fields and overgrown gardens — it is a common sight, with its black robber's mask and golden undersides.

It may take some coaxing to lure the yellowthroat into the open, though, because this is a bird that likes to stay deep in cover. It is also a curious, aggressive bird, fortunately, and squeaking or pishing usually brings the male out to the edge of the undergrowth, spoiling for a fight.

The male yellowthroat, with its mask and yellow throat and chest, is easy to identify. The female lacks noticeable field marks, being dull yellow below and olive above, but she shares her mate's short tail, which is often cocked up like a wren's. The male's song is a loud *whichity-whichity-whichity-which*, although it varies quite a bit from one region to the next. Both sexes give a sharp *tscheck* note when alarmed.

The yellowthroat's nest is fairly large, built near the ground in tussocks of grass or marsh vegetation and constructed of loosely woven leaves and grass blades. The four eggs, white with dark wreathing, take about 12 days to hatch, and the young stay with their parents for weeks after fledging — much longer than with most songbirds.

SPOTTER'S NOTES

- **Plumage** — Male, black mask, yellow underparts, olive back. Female, dull yellow below, olive above. Young male may have partial mask in fall.
- **Size** — 5 in (12 cms).
- **Behavior** — Scolds intruders, including people, but stays in thick cover near ground.
- **Habitat** — Brushy areas, especially wet or near water.

IDENTIFICATION

- **Song** — Loud *whichity-whichity-whichity-which*.
- **Food** — Insects.
- **Nest** — Bulky, woven of grass and leaves, built near ground in thick cover.
- **Eggs** — Usually 4; white with brownish wreathing.

Northern Cardinal
CARDINALIS CARDINALIS

Almost everyone knows the cardinal — even those who live outside its eastern and southern range. The male, with his bright red plumage, perky crest and black face, is one of the most instantly recognizable birds in North America.

The female is just as attractive, although not as conspicuous. Her plumage is buffy, with pink tones on the breast and touches on red on the crest, wings and tail. Both male and female have large, bright red bills, heavy enough to crack the strongest seeds with vise-like pressure.

The cardinal is a true garden bird, as commonly found around suburban homes as in country thickets. It enjoys sunflower seeds, and is easy to lure to a bird feeder, where its presence enlivens any snowy winter day. In New England and southern Canada, the cardinal pushes a little farther north each year, although it is most

SPOTTER'S NOTES

●● **Plumage** – Male, unmistakable: bright red overall, with red bill, black face and crest. Female buffy, with reddish crest bill, wings and tail.

●● **Size** – About 9 in (22 cms).

●● **Behavior** – Nervous, quick to give alarm.

●● **Habitat** – Yards, gardens, parks, brushy areas young woodlands.

IDENTIFICATION

●● **Song** – *What-cheer cheer cheer* or *who-it, who-it, who-it*.

●● **Food** – Insects, seeds, berries and fruit.

●● **Nest** – Made of twigs, bark strips, grass stems, weeds, often lined with hair.

●● **Eggs** – 3-5; pale bluish, heavily marked with brown.

common through the Mid-Atlantic region, Midwest and Plains, south to Florida and west to southern New Mexico.

Male cardinals are among the first birds to begin singing in the spring, frequently starting on mild days in February. The song is liquid, *what-cheer cheer cheer* or *who-it who-it who-it*, while both males and females give a distinctive *chip* call note when disturbed. The nest is built in shrubs, thickets, vine tangles or young trees, within 10 ft (3 m) of the ground. The eggs, which usually number four, are pale bluish with heavy brownish splotching. During the breeding season, male cardinals chase away other males, while females chase other females.

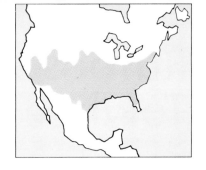

Blue Grosbeak
GUIRACA CAERULEA

The name "grosbeak" refers to this bird's enormous bill, which — like the cardinal's and many other finches' — is designed to crack seeds, a major part of the grosbeak's diet.

The blue grosbeak is found over the southern two-thirds of the U.S., overlapping the ranges of several other all- or mostly blue birds, which can lead to some confusion. The male blue grosbeak is bright blue, with a black face, dark wings and chestnut wingbars. The much smaller indigo bunting has no wingbars, while the eastern and western bluebirds have chestnut on the breast, not the wings. The female blue grosbeak is light brown, not blue, and has buffy wingbars. Young males are often blotched with blue and brown during the spring molt.

Blue grosbeaks are birds of thickets, hedgerows, brushy fields and stream banks, nesting in the lower branches of trees, especially sweet gum. The nest often incorporates one or more shed snake skins, and the grosbeaks may also pick up cellophane, perhaps mistaking it for a skin.

The male's song is a series of warbling notes that rise and fall in quick succession; the grosbeak also has a distinct call note, a metallic *chink!* Even when colors cannot be seen due to bad light, it is usually possible to see the flick of the grosbeak's tail — a behavioral field mark.

In warm weather, insects make up the bulk of what the blue grosbeak eats, but in fall the birds flock to grain and rice fields. They winter in Mexico, central America and Cuba.

SPOTTER'S NOTES
- **Plumage** – Male: Bright blue, black face, dark wings, chestnut wingbars. Female: Light brown, with buffy wingbars.
- **Size** – About 7 in (17 cms).
- **Behavior** – Perches on wires, fenceposts. Flicks and twitches tail.
- **Habitat** – Brushy areas, fencerows, tangles.

IDENTIFICATION
- **Song** – Rising and falling warble, also metallic alarm note.
- **Food** – Insects, seeds, grain.
- **Nest** – Deep cut of grass, leaves, bark; sometimes snakeskins.
- **Eggs** – Usually 4; pale blue or white.

Rufous-sided Towhee

PIPILO ERYTHROPHALMUS

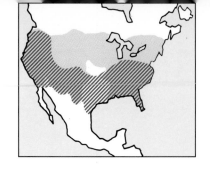

The towhee is usually heard before it is seen — and when it is looking for food, the noise it makes sound more like a large mammal than a small bird barely 8 in (20 cms) long.

The towhee is a ground feeder, searching for insects, invertebrates and seeds among the fallen leaves of the forest floor. These it uncovers by kicking backwards with both legs, scattering the leaves and making quite a ruckus.

A male rufous-sided towhee is a dapper bird — black head and back, long black tail with white corners, orangish sides and white belly. The female has a similar pattern, but is rusty brown where the male is black. Like the yellow-rumped warbler, the rufous-sided towhee was once divided into two species, because western birds have white wingbars and attractive white spots on the The songs are also different — a loud *drink-your-tea-a-a-a* in the East, and a variable *chup-chup-zee-e-e* in the West. Eastern birds have a readily identifiable *cher-WINK!* call note as well.

Towhees are absent from only a few areas of the Plains, breeding in deciduous forests and thickets in the East and West, and retreating only from the northernmost parts of their range in winter. They nest on or very near the ground, building a bowl of grass, leaves and twigs lined with fine shreds of grass. The eggs usually number from three to six, and are heavily dotted with cinnamon. Should you get too close to the nest, the female may run away through the grass like a rodent, or feign a broken wing like a killdeer.

SPOTTER'S NOTES

●● **Plumage** – Male: Black head, chest and upperparts; tail black with white corners and outer feathers. Rusty sides, white belly. Female brown instead of black.

●● **Size** – About 8½ in (21 cms).

●● **Behavior** – Ground feeder, scuffing leaves with both feet.

●● **Habitat** – Brushy woodlands, overgrown fields, fencerows, backyards.

I D E N T I F I C A T I O N

●● **Song** – *Drink-your-tea-a-a-a-a* in East; *chup-chup-zee-e-e* in West. Eastern call, loud *cher-WINK!*

●● **Food** – Insects, seeds, nuts, berries.

●● **Nest** – On or near ground; of grasses, weeds, leaves, twigs.

●● **Eggs** – 3–6; heavily spotted with cinnamon.

Song Sparrow
MELOSPIZA MELODIA

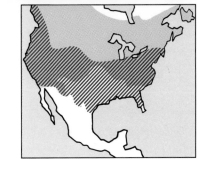

The song sparrow is a good example of how one species of animal can vary from place to place. Song sparrows everywhere have streaked breasts with a central spot (the best field mark), brownish plumage and long tails, but those from the Aleutians Islands in Alaska are large and dark gray, while song sparrows of the Southwest deserts are very pale. In the Pacific Northwest the overall color is rusty brown, while eastern birds are buffier.

Even the song varies a bit from region to region, although it usually takes the same basic form – three or four clear, whistled notes, followed by a trill.

Song sparrows are found over most of North America, except for the arctic; the do not breed in the Deep South or southern Plains, but do winter there commonly. They most often inhabit brushy, overgrown areas – old fields reverting to weeds and saplings, hedgerows, dense young woodlands, backyards. They stay near cover, but respond well to pishing or squeaking, sometimes coming very close. A song sparrow in flight is easy to identify because it pumps its long tail up and down as it flaps.

The female song sparrow is careful to hide her nest in thick grass, under shrubbery or on the ground in a tangle of briers. This does not fool a female cowbird, however, which will find the nest and substitute her eggs for the sparrows; only the yellow warbler suffers more from cowbird parasitism. Even though the baby cowbird quickly grows larger than its foster parents, the sparrows feed it as though it were their own – which is, of course, exactly what they think the cowbird chick is.

IDENTIFICATION

- **Song** – Three or four identical notes, followed by a trill.
- **Food** – Insects, seeds, berries.
- **Nest** – Cup of grass, leaves, weeds, on ground in thick cover.
- **Eggs** – 3–5; heavily spotted with reddish-brown.

SPOTTER'S NOTES
- **Plumage** – Brown above, white below, with streaked breast and dark central breast spot. Long tail, grayish eyebrow. Size and color varies from region to region.
- **Size** – 6–7 in (17 cms).
- **Behavior** – Pumps tail in flight.
- **Habitat** – Variety of brushy or overgrown habitats.

Chipping Sparrow
SPIZELLA PASSERINA

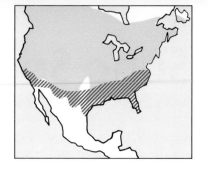

The chipping sparrow was always a common bird around farmhouses, collecting horse hair to line its tiny nest. And while it is still abundant in farmland, it has taken just as well to suburbia, nesting in shade trees, rose trellises, ornamental bushes – and lining its nest with dog hair, which is far easier to find today.

Identifying sparrows can be confusing, since the 33 North American species are all small, generally brownish birds. Small field marks become important; on the chipping sparrow, look for the combination of a reddish cap, white eyebrow, black line that goes through the eye, and a plain gray breast. The song is a machine-gunned series of high notes, all on the same pitch. The sexes are identical.

Chipping sparrows are found everywhere but the arctic and a small area of the southern Plains, and are year-round residents across most of the South and Southwest. In addition to backyards, they are found in fields, open woods and brushy lands – especially in the fall, when they form large flocks to migrate. In the winter, chipping sparrows

SPOTTER'S NOTES
- **Plumage** – Breeding adult: Rusty cap, white eyebrow, black eyeline, plain gray breast. Winter adult: Buffy, streaked cap.
- **Size** – 5½ in (13 cms).
- **Behavior** – Male sings from high perch. Often catches small insects on lawns.
- **Habitat** – Backyards, farmland, fields, brush, open woods.

IDENTIFICATION

- **Song** – Rapid string of single-pitch notes.
- **Food** – Insects, seeds.
- **Nest** – Small, tidy cup of fine grasses, weed stems, lined with hair.
- **Eggs** – 3–5; bluish with brown blotches at large end.

lose their rusty cap and white eyebrow, molting instead a cap of streaky buff.

The nest is made of very fine grasses and leaves, and is usually lined with hair. The eggs ordinarily number four, and are bluish with brown splotches at the large end.

Dark-Eyed Junco
JUNCO HYEMALIS

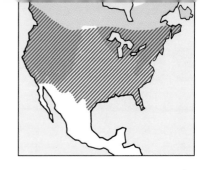

The junco is a sparrow, although with its gray plummage it may not look like one. Actually, how a junco looks varies widely, depending on where it lives. In the conifer forests of Canada, and down through New England and the Appalachians, juncos are plain gray, with white bellies. In the Black Hills of South Dakota, juncos are similar, but have white wing bars. In the Rockies and Pacific Coast states, the "Oregon" form is found, with a black hood, rusty back and sides, black wings and tail. Juncos in Arizona and New Mexico are completely gray, except for a rusty back. For a beginner, sorting them out can be confusing.

All juncos share one field mark that makes them easy to separate from other small birds — white outer tail feathers that flash as the birds flick their tails in flight. In most of the U.S., that sight is most common in the winter, when juncos migrate south, giving them the name of "snowbird." Wintering juncos stay in weedy fields, brushy areas, roadsides and woodland thickets, and will come to bird feeders in large numbers.

During the breeding season, juncos nest in coniferous or mixed forests, picking a spot hidden by an overhanging bank, fallen log or low bush; the nest is a cup of shredded bark, grass and root fibers built on the ground, sometimes in a shallow depression. The male's song is a trill, sung on a single pitch.

SPOTTER'S NOTES

●● **Plumage** – Varies widely, with females usually paler than males. All forms have white outer tail feathers.

●● **Size** – About 6 in (15 cms)

●● **Behavior** – Forms large flocks in winter.

●● **Habitat** – Coniferous or mixed forests in summer, fields and thickets in winter.

I D E N T I F I C A T I O N

●● **Song** – Trill, sung on single pitch.

●● **Food** – Weed seeds, insects.

●● **Nest** – On ground, concealed beneath overhang, log or shrub.

●● **Eggs** – 4–5; grayish with heavy brown wreathing at large end.

Bobolink

DOLICHONYX ORYZIVORUS

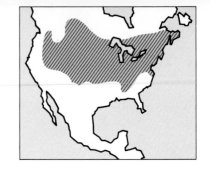

On the grasslands of the northern U.S. and southern Canada, the male bobolink's rolling song is the sound of spring. Fresh from South America, the males stake out their territories in hayfields, overgrown pastures and prairies, flying stiffly as they sing *bobolink-bobolink-bobolink-bobolink*. The females follow a week or two later, building their nests as part of a large, loose colony.

Males and females are strikingly different in appearance. The male is glossy black, with a triangular patch of buffy yellow on the nape of the neck, white wing patches and white rump. The female is buffy, with dark streaks and a dark-striped head. In the fall, the male molts into plumage very much like the female's, but as spring approaches, the tips of his feathers wear away, revealing his breeding colors underneath — a process called feather erosion.

In grassland regions the bobolink is a very common bird, although it has declined in the Northeast in recent years, because more and more hayfields are being cut early, while the bobolinks are still nesting. The nest itself is made of woven grass, hidden in thick vegetation, and the female never flies straight to it, but sneaks in and out on foot to confuse predators. Bobolinks lay an average of five eggs, which are among the prettiest of North American songbirds — cinnamon, with swirls and scrawls of darker brown.

IDENTIFICATION

- ●● **Song** – Rolling *bobolink-bobolink-bobolink-bobolink*.
- ●● **Food** – Insects, seeds, grain.
- ●● **Nest** – Made of grass, built on ground in thick cover.
- ●● **Eggs** – 4–7; cinnamon with brown scrawls and swirls.

SPOTTER'S NOTES

●● **Plumage** – Breeding male: Black, with yellowish neck patch, white rump and wing patches. Female and fall male: Buffy with brown streaks.

●● **Size** – About 7 in (17 cms).

●● **Behavior** – May nest in colonies. Males often sing in flight.

●● **Habitat** – Hayfields and grasslands; marshes and ricefields in migration.

Eastern and Western Meadowlarks

STURNELLA MAGNA and STURNELLA NEGLECTA

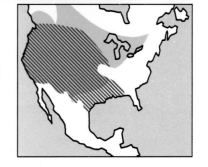

It takes a sharp eye to tell an eastern meadowlark from its western cousin on looks alone, because these two grassland birds are so similar. But when they open their mouths to sing, their songs are completely different, giving the bird-—watcher an easy way to tell them apart.

Why, you might wonder, are the meadowlarks considered different species (even though they look so much alike), when the many different junco phases are considered one variety? The answer is interbreeding; the juncos hybridize with each other, while the meadowlarks do not, even when they occur in the same field.

A meadowlark is a beautiful bird, with a rich yellow breast crossed by a black V, a streaky brown back and striped head. The tail is short, with white outer feathers that are displayed in flight. The western meadowlark is somewhat paler than the eastern, with a touch more yellow on the face. The songs, as mentioned, are the key to identification – a clear *spring-of-the-year* for the eastern, and a series of up to 10 flute-like phrases for the western.

Eastern meadowlarks are found from Maine and Quebec to Minnesota, Nebraska and the Southwest, while the western ranges from the Great Lakes region and Canadian prairies to the Gulf and Pacific coasts. There are many locations where both species are found, but where that happens, the eastern prefers moist areas like wet meadows, and the western drier, upland habitat.

SPOTTER'S NOTES

●● **Plumage** – Yellow breast with black V, brown, streaked upperparts, striped head, short tail with white outer feathers. Sexes identical. Western paler, with more yellow on face.

●● **Size** – 9 in (22 cms).

●● **Behavior** – Sings from wires, fenceposts. Flies with wings held level, with stiff flaps.

●● **Habitat** – Open country – pastures, meadows, prairies.

IDENTIFICATION

●● **Song** – Eastern: whistled *spring-of-the-year*. Western: 7–10 flute-like phrases.

●● **Food** – Insects and seeds.

●● **Nest** – Depression in ground lined with grass, then roofed over with woven grass arch (both species).

●● **Eggs** – 3–5; white with purplish-brown spots (both species).

Red-Winged Blackbird

AGELAIUS PHOENICEUS

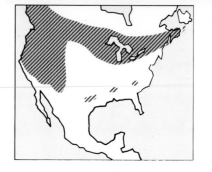

It is hard to miss a red-winged blackbird. This denizen of the marshes and grasslands is so loud, so conspicuous, that even non-birders take note of it.

A year-round resident in all but the northern U.S. and Canada (where it is a summer bird only), the red-winged blackbird is one of the 10 most common birds on the continent. Almost every marsh, swamp, tidal flat, wet meadow, hayfield and grassy orchard has a small colony, squabbling and chasing each other with springtime energy. The glossy black males sing from prominent perches like utility wires, cattail stalks and fenceposts, a creaky *ok-a-lee-e-e-e-e* that is accompanied by a flaring of his red wing patches, edged with yellow.

The females are harder to see, since they are heavily streaked with dark brown, and stay lower in the marsh vegetation. Immature males resemble their mothers, but have a small red wing patch.

Red-wings nest in colonies that may number into the thousands, although each pair vigorously defends a small territory around their nest, which is woven of grass and weed leaves in a clump of marsh vegetation, just above the water. Frequently, a male will have several mates within his territory, and he chases away any other males that come too close.

In central California, there is a color form of the standard red-wing that has solid red patches, with no yellow borders. A separate species, the tri-colored blackbird, is also found in California; it has red epaulets with white, rather than yellow, edges.

I D E N T I F I C A T I O N

- **Song** – Creaky *ok-a-lee-e-e-e-e*!
- **Food** – Mostly insects; also some seeds.
- **Nest** – Built in clump of reeds over water; woven cup of grass and weed leaves.
- **Eggs** – 3 or 4; pale bluish-green with dark swirls and scrawls.

SPOTTER'S NOTES

- **Plumage** – Male: Glossy black with red epaulets, edged with yellow. Female: Brown with heavy streaking, no red.
- **Size** – About 8½ in (21 cms).
- **Behavior** – Males may try to chase people wearing bright red clothing. Forms immense winter flocks.
- **Habitat** – Almost any wetland area; also increasingly in hayfields, orchards, other upland sites.

Brown-Headed Cowbird

MOLOTHRUS ATER

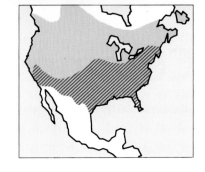

Among bird-watchers, the brown-headed cowbird has an unsavory reputation because it is a nest parasite, throwing out the eggs of other birds and laying its own in the nest, then abandoning them. The foster parents, unaware that a switch has taken place, raise the cowbird's chicks as their own.

The cowbirds developed this strange behavior over thousands of years, when the Plains of North America supported vast herds of bison. The cowbird flocks followed the bison, feeding on the insects the herds stirred up. But because the herds constantly moved, the cowbirds couldn't stay in one place for a month or more to nest, incubate and raise chicks. So they took to nest parasitism.

Today, the big bison herds are gone, and cowbirds associate with cattle, which do not migrate. The cowbirds still parasitize other birds out of instinct, however, and with the change from forests to farms in the East, the cowbird is found in many regions where it was absent in the past. This may be contributing to declines in some songbirds like vireos, warblers and flycatchers.

SPOTTER'S NOTES

●● **Plumage** – Male: Brown head and glossy black body. Female: Plain brown.

●● **Size** – 7 in (17 cms).

●● **Behavior** – Nest parasite; female slips into unoccupied nest, throws out owner's eggs and lays one of hers.

●● **Habitat** – Suburbs, parks, farmland, fields. Especially around farmyards for spilled grain.

I D E N T I F I C A T I O N

●● **Song** – Squeaky, three-noted call; also a flight call with a high squeal and two lower notes.

●● **Food** – Insects, seeds, grain.

●● **Nest** – Builds none.

●● **Eggs** – Up to 6 in different nests; off-white spotted with brown.

Cowbirds are fairly drab in color. A male has a brown head and a glossy black body, while the female is plain brown. Both have relatively short tails and short, conical beaks – much shorter than grackles or starlings. They flock around farms, fields and cow pastures, in huge numbers.

Common Grackle
QUISCALUS QUISCULA

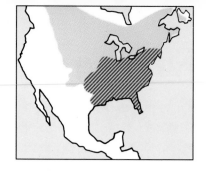

For most people, a grackle is just a "blackbird," not as pretty as a cardinal or a robin, a bird to mostly just ignore. But a male grackle, strutting proudly across a yard with his black feathers shining purple, green and bronze in the sun, staring out at the world with sharp yellow eyes, is really a very attractive bird.

Grackles are common over most of southern and eastern Canada, and in the U.S. from the Rockies and southern Plains to the Gulf and Atlantic coasts. They are very much suburban birds, abundant in parks, housing developments and towns, as well as in open countryside, wetlands, farms and open woods. They breed in small colonies of up to 50 pairs, often in groves of shade trees or conifers, and in winter will flock with red-winged blackbirds, cowbirds and

starlings in nighttime roosts that comprise millions of birds.

The sexes are similar, although males have longer tails and glossy heads (brownish in females). In flight, the male's long tail is held in a peculiar keel-shape, with the edges rising above the center — an excellent field mark. Young grackles are dull brown, with dark brown eyes. The bill is very long, much more so than in other blackbirds.

Grackles are omnivores, eating a wide variety of food — insects, worms, seeds, berries, fruit, bird eggs and chicks, small frogs, salamanders and snakes. They often forage on grassy lawns, moving with a jerky strut.

There are two other, larger grackles in the U.S. The boat-tailed grackle is found near the coast from New York to Texas, while the great-tailed grackle, up to 18 in (45 cms) long, ranges across the southern Plains and Southwest.

IDENTIFICATION

- **Song** – Raspy, creaking notes. Call a harsh *chack*.
- **Food** – Wide variety of plant and animal matter.
- **Nest** – Colonial; nest large bowl of grass, weeds, often high in tree.
- **Eggs** – 5–6; pale greenish or yellowish with brown spots and scrawls.

SPOTTER'S NOTES
- **Plumage** – Adults glossy black with long tails, yellow eyes; some males have purplish gloss, others bronze. Females browner, with shorter tail.
- **Size** – About 12 in (30 cms).
- **Behavior** – Spends much time foraging on the ground.
- **Habitat** – Towns, suburbs, open country, wetlands.

Northern Oriole
ICTERUS GALBULA

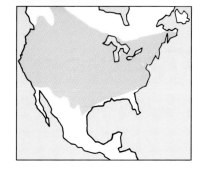

The oriole's nest is justly famous for its beauty and engineering. The female takes a week or more to complete the job, starting by looping and knotting long pieces of plant fibers, string, bark strips and hair over a forked tree branch. More strands are added, woven together to form a hanging basket that gently cradles the eggs 30 or 40 ft (9 or 12 m) above the ground. For some reasons, orioles are fond of placing their nests over water (such as in a tree growing beside a river) or over macadam roads.

There are two distinct forms of the northern oriole, once thought to be separate species. The "Baltimore" oriole of the East has a black hood, back, wings and tail, with orange on the undersides, rump and tail patches. The male "Bullock's" oriole of the West is similar, but has an orange face and eyebrow, and a large white wing patch. The females of both forms are duller — greenish-orange in the East, gray-green in the West. In the Great Plains, the two forms hybridize freely.

The eastern male's song is a lovely series of *hew-lee* notes that bubbles and gurgles, while the "Bullock's" male's song is similar, but faster and less musical. The males are very much in evidence in spring, chasing each other through the high treetops, flashing orange in the sun. Northern orioles like open woodlands (especially along rivers and streams) as well as shaded neighborhoods, tree-lined lanes, parks and orchards. Elm trees are a particular favorite. The oriole's diet is made up primarily of insects, but they also eat fruit and nectar. They can be attracted to feeders with pieces of oranges, as well as with special nectar feeders, similar to hummingbird feeders.

SPOTTER'S NOTES

●● **Plumage** – Males: Bold orange and black pattern; eastern males have black hood, western males orange face and eyebrow with white wing patch. Females greenish or green-orange.

●● **Size** – About 8 in (20 cms).

●● **Behavior** – Stays in treetops, sometimes swooping out to catch insects.

●● **Habitat** – Deciduous trees, especially along waterways.

IDENTIFICATION

●● **Song** – Rich series of *hew-lee* notes and other phrases; faster, harsher in western birds.

●● **Food** – Insects, fruit, nectar.

●● **Nest** – Hanging basket of woven plant fibers; western nests not as deep or hanging.

●● **Eggs** – 4–5; pale gray with intricate dark scrawls.

Western Tanager

PIRANGA LUDOVICIANA

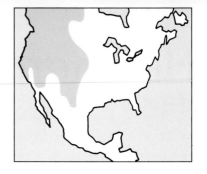

In the conifer forests of the western mountains, no bird is prettier than the male western tanager, with his flame-red head, yellow body and black wings and tail. Against the backdrop of dark green fir and pine needles, he simply glows.

The tanagers are a tropical family, with four North American species, all beautiful. The western tanager ranges from the Northwest Territories to the Mexican border, while the scarlet tanager (bright red with black wings and tail) is northeastern in distribution. The all-red summer tanager is southern and southwestern, while the hepatic tanager is confined to mountain forests in the Southwest.

The female western tanager – as with all female tanagers – is dull yellowish-green. At the end of the breeding season, before migrating to Mexico or Central America for the winter, the male molts out of his brilliant courtship plumage and into a pattern very much like his mate's.

Nesting occurs in conifer trees, with the shallow bowl of pine twigs and grass built on a horizontal branch 30-60 ft (9-12 m) above the ground. The eggs are blue-green, with dark spots

SPOTTER'S NOTES

- **Plumage** – Breeding male: red-orange head, yellow body, black wings and tail with yellow wingbars. Female and winter male: Yellowish with dark wings and tail.
- **Size** – 7 in (17 cms).
- **Behavior** – Feeds quietly in tree branches; hard to spot despite colors.
- **Habitat** – Coniferous forests; sometimes mixed or deciduous woods.

IDENTIFICATION

- **Song** – Robin-like string of notes, with a pause between phrases.
- **Food** – Insects, some fruits and buds.
- **Nest** – Shallow bowl of twigs, grasses, on high conifer branch.
- **Eggs** – 3–5; blue-green, with dark spots mostly at large end.

at the large end. The eggs hatch in about two weeks, and the chicks stay in the nest for another 14 days – about the same schedule most songbirds keep. The nestlings are fed insects, but when they mature they will add some fruit to their diet.

House Sparrow
PASSER DOMESTICUS

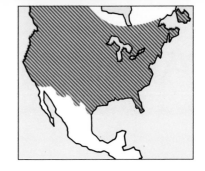

An import from Europe like the starling, the house sparrow has been almost as successful, spreading over all of the U.S. and most of southern Canada since it was first released in the 1850s.

Originally, the house sparrow was brought to North America to help control insect pests, but it soon became a pest itself, as so many alien species do. It is aggressive, taking over nest sites from bluebirds, purple martins and other native birds. At the turn of the century the house sparrow was at its most abundant, feeding on grain spilled around farms, or picked from horse manure in the cities. The introduction of the automobile brought a decline in its numbers, but it is still common wherever people live.

The male has a gray crown, black throat and chest, chestnut neck nape, gray undersides and brown wings, while the female is brown above and gray below, with buffy eyebrows. In winter

SPOTTER'S NOTES
●● **Plumage** – Male: Black throat and chest, brown back, gray undersides, face and crown. Female: Brown above, gray below, buffy eyebrows.
●● **Size** – About 6 in (15 cms).

●● **Behavior** – Noisy, aggressive to other small birds.
●● **Habitat** – Near human habitation, from farms to cities.

the male's black bill turns yellowish, and his black chest patch shrinks to a small area on the chin. The song, heard all year but most commonly in spring, is an unmusical jumble of chirps and twitters.

House sparrows are cavity nesters, but are not picky about the openings, taking over chimneys, drainpipes, birdboxes and openings in the eaves of houses. The nest is a collection of straw, grass, weeds, feathers, paper and other trash, often filling the available space. The five to seven eggs are off-white, with heavy brown spotting.

House sparrows eat a variety of insects, seeds, fruits and berries, and can take over bird feeders. In city parks they sometimes become panhandlers, begging for food from people, or scavenging scraps from garbage cans.

I D E N T I F I C A T I O N

●● **Song** – Jumble of chirps and twitters.
●● **Food** – Insects, seeds, grain, fruit, berries, human trash.
●● **Nest** – Large collection of straw, grass, weeds, feathers, debris; in cavity.
●● **Eggs** – Usually 5–7; off-white with brown spotting.

American Goldfinch
CARDUELIS TRISTIS

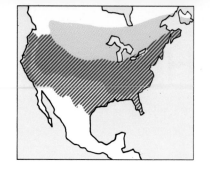

The American goldfinch goes by lots of names, most of them descriptive – wild canary, yellowbird, thistle-bird, even catnip bird, because it eats the seeds of catnip plants. But "goldfinch" sums it up rather well – a small, bright yellow sprite of the fields, thickets and meadows.

In summer, the American goldfinch is found in southern Canada and the northern two-thirds of the U.S.; in winter, it drops south, from New England and the Great Lakes to the Plains, Southwest and Pacific coast. The male also undergoes a remarkable transformation. His winter plumage is very much like the female's: dull olive, with faint yellow on the head. But as winter progresses, his feather tips wear away to reveal his breeding plumage underneath, shining yellow, a black cap, and black wings and tail with white wingbars. The female becomes only slightly brighter, staying mostly olive year-round.

The American goldfinch is one of the latest-—nesting songbirds in North America, waiting until the thistles go to seed in late summer so they can use the soft thistle-down to build their cups. A goldfinch nest is usually placed in the upright crotch of a sapling or small tree growing in a brushy field or fencerow; the plant down is often covered with a layer of cobwebs or caterpillar silk, and the finished nest is very neat in appearance. The normal clutch is five eggs, which are unmarked white or very pale blue.

Goldfinches are common feeder birds, although they require a smaller seed than bigger songbirds like cardinals. In the wild they eat the seeds of thistles, mints and other fine-seeded plants.

SPOTTER'S NOTES
●● **Plumage** – Breeding male: Bright yellow body, black cap, tail and wings, white wingbars. Female brighter yellow in spring.
●● **Size** – 5 in (12 cms).
●● **Behavior** – Characteristic rising and falling flight.
●● **Habitat** – Meadows, overgrown fields, thickets. Fields in winter.

I D E N T I F I C A T I O N

●● **Song** – Clear, light warble. Flight call thin *per-chick-o-ree* between wingbeats.
●● **Food** – Small seeds and berries, insects.
●● **Nest** – Small, neat cup of plant down in upright crotch of sapling.
●● **Eggs** – 3–6; white or pale bluish.

OIL SUNFLOWER

* Chickadee
  Mourning Dove
  Goldfinch
* House Finch
* Purple Finch
  Grackle
* Evening Grosbeak
  Steller's Jay
  Dark-eyed Junco
* White-breasted Nuthatch
  Pine Siskin
  Redpoll
  Red-winged Blackbird
  House Sparrow
  Song Sparrow
* White-crowned Sparrow
* White-throated Sparrow
  Tufted Titmouse
  Woodpeckers

THISTLE (Niger)

  Brown-headed Cowbird
* Goldfinch
  House Finch
  Mourning Dove
  Purple Finch
  Dark-eyed Junco
* Pine Siskin
  House Sparrow
  Song Sparrow
  White-throated Sparrow

SUNFLOWER CHIPS

  Chickadee
  Brown-headed Cowbird
  Mourning Dove
  Goldfinch
  Grackle
  House Finch
  House Sparrow
* Pine Siskin
  Red-winged Blackbird
  White-throated Sparrow

STRIPED SUNFLOWER

  Chickadee
  House Finch
  Purple Finch
  Grackle
  Evening Grosbeak
* Steller's Jay
  White-breasted Nuthatch
  House Sparrow
  White-throated Sparrow
  White-crowned Sparrow
* Tufted Titmouse
* Red-bellied Woodpecker

CRACKED CORN

  Mourning Dove
  Rock Dove
  Grackle
  Blue Jay
  Dark-eyed Junco
  Red-winged Blackbird
  House Sparrow
  Tree Sparrow
  White-throated Sparrow
  Starling
  Red-bellied Woodpecker

PEANUT KERNELS

  Chickadee
* Blue Jay
  White-breasted Nuthatch
  House Sparrow
* Tufted Titmouse
  Woodpeckers

PEANUT HEARTS

  Brown-headed Cowbird
  Dark-eyed Junco
  White-throated Sparrow
* Starling

SAFFLOWER

  (Squirrels, grackles & blackbirds don't eat)
  Chickadee
  Mourning Dove
  House Finch
  Steller's Jay
  White-breasted Nuthatch
  House Sparrow
  Tufted Titmouse
  Red-bellied Woodpecker

WHITE MILLET

* Brown-headed Cowbird
* Mourning Dove
* Dark-eyed Junco
  Red-winged Blackbird
  Pine Siskin
* House Sparrow
* Song Sparrow
* Tree Sparrow
  White-crowned Sparrow
  White-throated Sparrow
* Starling
  Rufous- sided Towhee
  Varied Thrush

RED MILLET

  Same list as for white millet, but generally not as well liked.

DELUXE BLEND by
Wild Birds Nature Shop
The same birds that are attracted to Oil Sunflower, Striped Sunflower, Safflower, and White Millet.

WOODLAND MIX by
Wild Birds Nature Shop
The same birds that are attracted to Oil Sunflower, White Millet and Red Millet.

Compliments of

Wild Birds Nature Shop

HUMMINGBIRD FEEDERS

Darting and dashing among the flowers in your garden, enjoy the antics and wonder of the mighty hummingbirds. Ask for our hummingbird nectar recipe!

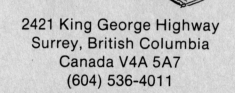

2421 King George Highway
Surrey, British Columbia
Canada V4A 5A7
(604) 536-4011

Wild Birds Nature Shop

House Finch
CARPODACUS MEXICANUS

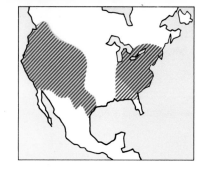

A native of the West, the house finch has been a resident of the East for less than 50 years, following the escape on Long Island of birds being kept illegally for the pet trade. In its new home the house finch has thrived, and is now found in cities, towns and farmland from Ontario to Florida and the Midwest. It seem only a matter of time until it expands westward and meets the native population at the edge of the prairies.

House finches do best around people, nesting in shrubs and ornamental trees, and patronizing bird feeders for sunflower seeds. Interestingly, when house finches move into an area, the number of house sparrows drops, probably from increased competition.

Male house finches are brownish, with a cardinal-red chest, face and rump; the similar purple finch of the North is a duller cranberry red. The female house finch is dusky brown, with dark brown streaks on the head, back and breast, and lacks the female purple finch's light eyebrow. In winter house finches form large flocks, especially around bird feeders, although they break into pairs for the breeding season. The male's song is a lively warble that usually ends with *cher-urr*.

SPOTTER'S NOTES

- **Plumage** – Male: Brownish, with red face, chest and rump. Female dusky brown, with streaking on head, back, breast.
- **Size** – About 6 in (15 cms).
- **Behavior** – Forms flocks in winter.
- **Habitat** – Semi-arid areas in West, around human habitation, farmland in East.

I D E N T I F I C A T I O N

- **Song** – Lively warble ending with *cher-urr*.
- **Food** – Insects, seeds, berries.
- **Nest** – Grass, leaves, twigs, hair.
- **Eggs** – 4–5; pale bluish with brown spots or wreathing.

One reason the house finch has done so well may be that it is not picky about a place for its nest – it will build in shrubs and low trees, climbing vines, even in the old nests of other birds. It has a special fondness for hanging baskets of houseplants, and will dig a shallow hole in the soil, then line it with grass. Wreaths on front doors, and outdoor light fixtures, are also common spots for house finch nests.

Quiz

Blue jay

Eastern phoebe

1. What are bird feathers made of?

2. What is the function of down?

3. What are three weight-reducing adaptations in a bird's body?

4. Name one reason a male bird sings.

5. Is a song more or less complex than a call?

6. Do all birds build nests?

7. What is it called when a young bird leaves the nest for the first time?

8. What are some ways birds have of navigating on migration?

9. What is a field mark?

10. In 7×35 binoculars, what does the 7 refer to?

11. What is the best all-around food for a bird feeder?

12. How soon after hatching can Canada goose chicks feed themselves?

13. What time of the year is a drake mallard in 'eclipse' plumage?

14. What color is a male wood duck's eye?

15. What does a killdeer use for a nest?

16. When a baby herring gull is hungry, what part of its parent's beak does it peck?

17. What are soaring hawks like red-tails called?

18. Where is the ring-necked pheasant originally from?

19. What is a bobwhite quail flock called?

20. A mourning dove pair will raise up to how many broods a season?

21. Which owl has the widest distribution?

22. Eastern screech-owls come in two color phases. What are they?

23. What produces the booming sound that male nighthawks make in their courtship flight?

24. Ants are the preferred food of which common woodpecker?

25. What is the color difference between a male and female downy woodpecker?

26. Phoebes often cover the outsides of their nests with what material?

27. Of what material is a blue jay's nest primarily made?

28. Are black-billed magpies more or less intelligent than most birds?

29. What is the proper name for habitat along a waterway like a stream?

30. How does a crow react when it spots a great horned owl?

31. What is the European name for a chickadee?

32. Why does a nuthatch go down a tree head-first?

33. What do white-breasted nuthatches crush around their nest holes, perhaps to drive away predators?

34. What two introduced birds steal eastern bluebird nest sites?

35. What material do wood thrushes almost always use as a base for their nests?

36. To what group of birds does the American robin belong?

37. What are two good foods for attracting northern mockingbirds to a feeder?

38. What year was the European starling first introduced to New York City?

39. Why is the red-eyed vireo sometimes called the 'preacher bird'?

40. Which warbler winters the farthest north?

41. In which direction is the northern cardinal's range expanding?

42. Which towhees have white wingbars — eastern or western birds?

43. What does a song sparrow do in flight that

Common grackle

makes it easy to identify?

44. What material does a chipping sparrow use to line its nest?

45. Do western and eastern meadowlarks hybridize?

46. Do male red-winged blackbirds always have one mate?

47. How did the brown-headed cowbird adapt its breeding behavior to following the bison herds?

48. What shape does a northern oriole's nest take?

49. Why was the house sparrow brought to North America?

50. Why does the American goldfinch delay nesting until late summer?

Black-capped chickadee

Mallard

Further Reading

At the turn of the century, most people studied birds over the barrel of a shotgun, shooting specimens for identification. Today, birders rely on field guides, which point out the field marks, songs and ranges of each species. There are many excellent guides on the market. Among the best are:

A Field Guide to the Birds, by Roger Tory Peterson (Houghton Mifflin), was the first of the true field guides. In two volumes (eastern and western), both recently revised, it is justly known as the 'Birder's Bible'.

A Field Guide to the Birds of North America, published by the National Geographic Society, includes all of North America's birds in one 465-page book. More attention is paid to subspecies and color forms, and the range maps are opposite the illustration, rather than in the back of the book as with Peterson's.

Birds of North America (Golden Press), by Robbins, Bruun and Zimm, shares the advantages of full-continent coverage and handier range maps although the illustrations and maps are not always as clear.

RIGHT: Young birds do not always look like their parents. This young robin will have a spotted breast until early fall, when it will molt a solid-orange breast like its parents.

LEFT: Field marks, like the red breast of this adult robin, are colors, plumage patterns or shapes that are easily recognizable, allowing a birder to identify the species from a distance.

The Audubon Society Field Guide to North American Birds (Knopf), a two-volume softbound set, uses color photographs instead of paintings. Unfortunately, the photos are of uneven quality, which makes identification difficult. It is also arranged by color and shape instead of family, making its use even less convenient.

The Audubon Society Master Guide to Birding (Knopf), a three-volume set, uses photos and artwork to excellent effect. A reference work rather than a field guide, it is for experienced birders.

The Peterson Field Guide Series of which the two general bird guides are a part, also includes the following volumes on birding specialties:
Birds of Texas and Adjacent States — Peterson
Birds Nests (East of the Mississippi) — Harrison
Birds Nests (West of the Mississippi) — Harrison
Hawks — Clark and Wheeler

Useful Organizations

An interest in birds usually leads to a concern for the environment as a whole. For more information about environmental protection, contact one of the following organizations:

National Audubon Society
950 Third Ave.
New York, NY 10022

National Wildlife Federation
1412 Sixteenth St. NW
Washington, D.C. 20036

World Wildlife Fund
1255 23rd St. NW
Washington, D.C. 20037

American Birding Association
Box 6599
Colorado Springs, CO 80934

The Sierra Club
730 Polk St.
San Francisco, CA 94109

Friends of the Earth
530 Seventh St. SE
Washington D.C. 20003

The Nature Conservancy
1815 North Lynn St.
Arlington, VA 22209

ABOVE: Among many birds, the male is the more colorful of the pair, to help him attract a mate and drive off rivals. This orange and black beauty is a male northern oriole.

Index

62

Acknowledgments

Key tr = Top Right; br = Bottom Right; bl = Bottom Left.

© Gregory K Scott: Pages 3, 4, 5, 6, 7, 8, 9, 10, 11, 12, 13tr, 14, 16, 18bl, 21, 22, 23, 24, 25, 26, 28, 29, 30, 31, 32, 33, 34, 35, 37, 38, 40, 41, 42, 44, 45, 46, 47, 48, 49, 50, 52, 53, 55, 56, 58, 59, 60tr & bl. © Scott Weidensaul: Pages 13br, 18br, 57, 60tr, 64. © Wayne Lankinen Pages 15 & 39. © Vernon Eugene Grove Jr: Pages 17 & 20. © Joe McDonald: Pages 19 & 36. © Anthony Mercieca: Pages 43 & 54. © Edgar T Jones: Page 51.

ABOVE: A male bluebird delivers a grub to its nest box; such artificial nest sites are easy to build, and are a good way to help cavity-nesting birds.

RIGHT: Hundreds of Canada geese line the edge of the ice at a municipal reservoir. Parks and watersheds offer good birding possibilities, usually close to home.

Answers

1. Keratin **2.** Insulation **3.** Light bones, air sacs, light beak. **4.** Attract mate, define territory, scare off rivals. **5.** More complex. **6.** No. **7.** Fledging. **8.** Using sun and stars, wind direction, landmarks. **9.** Unique identifying features of each species. **10.** Magnification. **11.** "Oil" sunflower seed. **12.** Immediately. **13.** Late summer. **14.** Red. **15.** A depression in rocky, gravelly soil. **16.** The red spot. **17.** Buteos. **18.** The Orient. **19.** A covey. **20.** 6. **21.** The great horned owl – North and South America. **22.** Reddish-brown and gray. **23.** Air rushing over the primary feathers. **24.** Common flicker. **25.** Male has a small spot of red on the back of the head. **26.** Moss. **27.** Twigs. **28.** More intelligent. **29.** Riparian habitat. **30.** Calls other crows to mob the owl. **31.** Tit. **32.** To find insects other birds missed. **33.** Insects. **34.** European starling, house sparrow. **35.** Leaves. **36.** Thrushes. **37.** Cracked corn and raisins. **38.** 1890. **39.** Because it sings constantly through the day. **40.** Yellow-rumped warbler. **41.** To the north. **42.** Western. **43.** Pumps its tail in flight. **44.** Hair or fur. **45.** No. **46.** No. **47.** By laying its eggs in the nests of other species. **48.** A hanging basket. **49.** To control insect pests. **50.** To wait for the thistles to go to seed.